AF835655

Code of practice for legal admissibility and evidential weight of information communicated electronically

Code of practice for legal admissibility and evidential weight of information communicated electronically

Peter Howes
Alan Shipman

Business
Information

While every care has been taken in developing and compiling the recommendations herein, as a recommended code of practice for legal admissibility and evidential weight of information communicated electronically, the authors and contributing organizations accept no liability for any loss or damage caused, arising directly or indirectly in connection with reliance on its contents except to the extent that such liability may not lawfully be excluded.

First edition published 1998 (PD 5000)

Second edition 2002 (PD 5000)

Third edition 2005

BIP 0008-2

ISBN 0 580 45672 2

Contents

Foreword		**ix**
Acknowledgements		**xi**
Introduction		**1**
	Information communications	1
	Purpose of the Code	2
	Management framework	2
	Plan-Do-Check-Act model	5
General		**7**
	Scope	7
	Applicability	8
	The users	8
	Objectives	8
	Compliance	8
	Key requirements	9
	Trusted third party services	9
	Recipient's perspective	10
	Documentation	11
Chapter 1	**Information communications policy**	**13**
1.1	Management overview	13
1.2	Information communications policy document	13
1.2.1	Structure	13
1.2.2	Communications	13
1.2.3	Compression	15
1.2.4	Encryption	16
1.2.5	Procedures	16
1.2.6	Delivery/receipt	17
1.2.7	Responsibility	17
Chapter 2	**Duty of care**	**19**
2.1	Management overview	19
2.2	Security management guidance	19
2.3	Information security management	21

2.3.1 Security elements 21
2.3.2 Information security policy 21
2.3.3 Risk assessment 22
2.3.4 Information security infrastructure 23
2.4 Business continuity planning 23
2.5 Third parties 25
2.6 Information security principles 27
2.6.1 General 27
2.6.2 Confidentiality 28
2.6.3 Integrity 28
2.6.4 Availability 29
2.7 Consultations 29

Chapter 3 Procedures and processes 31

3.1 Management overview 31
3.2 Procedures manual 31
3.2.1 Documentation 31
3.2.2 Content 31
3.2.3 Compliance with procedures 32
3.2.4 Updating and reviews 32
3.3 Preparation for communication 33
3.3.1 General 33
3.3.2 Malicious software 33
3.3.3 File compression 34
3.3.4 File encryption 35
3.3.5 Sender identity 39
3.3.6 Integrity information 39
3.3.7 Data file format exchange 39
3.3.8 Storage 40
3.3.9 Destruction 41
3.3.10 Transfers to archives 42
3.4 Communication 42
3.4.1 Systems 42
3.5 Receipt of communication 44
3.5.1 General 44
3.5.2 Malicious software 44
3.5.3 Decompression 45
3.5.4 Decryption 45
3.5.5 Sender identity 46
3.5.6 Integrity verification 46
3.5.7 Confirmation of receipt 48
3.5.8 Data file format exchange 49
3.5.9 Storage 50
3.6 System maintenance 51
3.7 Security and protection 51
3.8 Contracts 51
3.9 Third parties 52
3.10 Standardized documents 53
3.11 Version control 54
3.12 Change control 55

Chapter 4 Enabling technologies **57**
4.1 Management overview 57
4.2 System description manual 57
4.2.1 Documentation 57
4.2.2 Content 58
4.3 General issues 58
4.4 Communications systems 60
4.5 Access levels 60
4.5.1 General 60
4.5.2 Access levels and third parties 61
4.6 Identity authentication 61
4.7 Identification of documents 62
4.8 Communication initiation 63
4.9 Integrity checks 64
4.9.1 Sending 64
4.9.2 Receiving 68
4.9.3 Sending data to archives 68
4.10 Sender and recipient authentication 69
4.11 Receipt confirmation 69
4.11.1 General 69
4.11.2 Document details 70
4.11.3 Receipt details 70
4.12 Interim or temporary document storage 71
4.13 Time considerations 71
4.14 Error handling processes 72
Chapter 5 Audit trails **73**
5.1 Management overview 73
5.2 Audit trails 73
5.2.1 Historical records 73
5.2.2 Audit trail data 74
5.2.3 Content 74
5.2.4 Access 74
5.3 Managing audit trails 74
5.3.1 General 74
5.3.2 Storage and retention 75
5.3.3 Format 75
5.3.4 Access and interpretation 76
5.3.5 Audit trail information 76
5.3.6 Compliance 77
5.3.7 Statement of compliance 78
5.3.7.1 General 78
5.3.7.2 End user organizations 78
5.3.7.3 System integrators and developers 78
5.3.7.4 System auditors 78
5.4 Audit trail content 79
5.4.1 General 79
5.4.2 Generation 79
5.4.3 System audit trail 80

5.5 Communicated information 80
5.5.1 General 80
5.5.2 Route details 80
5.5.3 Storage requirements 80
5.5.4 Date and time 81
5.6 Security 81
5.6.1 General 81
5.6.2 Access 81
5.6.3 Integrity and protection 82

Chapter 6 Unstructured message considerations 83

6.1 General 83
6.2 Policy objectives 83
6.3 Creation 84
6.4 Spamming, filtering and viruses 85
6.5 Copyright and personal use 86
6.5.1 Policy 86
6.5.2 Copyright 87
6.5.3 Privacy 87
6.5.4 Personal use 87
6.5.5 Monitoring 87
6.5.6 Breaches, procedures and penalties 88
6.6 Retention and destruction 88
6.7 Receipt 89

Annex A Example electronic communications policy 91

Annex B References 86

Foreword

This *Code of practice for legal admissibility and evidential weight of information communicated electronically* (referred to in this document as 'the Code') is primarily concerned with the authenticity, integrity and availability of electronically communicated information, to the demonstrable levels of certainty required by an organization. It is particularly applicable where this communicated information may be used as evidence in disputes inside and outside the legal system.

This is the third edition of the Code, which was first published by BSI in 1999, as PD 5000. This edition is a structural, technical and editorial revision of the second edition (PD 5000:2002), which is now superseded. PD 5000 was published in five parts:

- Part 1, *Information stored electronically* (PD 0008:1999);
- Part 2, *Electronic communications and email policy*;
- Part 3, *Identity, signature and copyright*;
- Part 4, *Using certification authorities*;
- Part 5, *Using trusted third party archives.*

This third edition is now renumbered as the second part of BIP 0008, which is made up of the following publications, with the general title *Code of practice for legal admissibility and evidential weight*:

- BIP 0008-1:2004, *Information stored electronically*;
- BIP 0008-2:2005, *Information communicated electronically*;
- BIP 0008-3:2005, *Linking electronic identity to documents.*

Users of the first and second editions of PD 5000 should consider the advantages of assessing their information management systems in the light of this new version, and amend their systems and/or documentation where appropriate.

This document is published by BSI in recognition of the large number of implementations of electronic information management systems, and of the continuing uncertainty about the legal acceptability of information that has been communicated electronically. It provides good practice guidance for electronic communication of information.

Acknowledgements

The editors would like to thank the BSI Legal Admissibility Editorial Board and EOI Ltd for their business foresight in the development of this Code of practice.

In particular, special thanks go to Roger Peggram, Valerie Cumming and Mike Brewer for their many helpful comments in the drafting of this publication and their suggestions for improvements.

Finally, we would like to thank Simone Levy from BSI for her help in getting this project off the ground and Jenny Cranwell for her excellent advice and copy editing skills.

Peter Howes (Editor)

Alan Shipman (Editor)

Group 5 Training Limited

The first version of PD 5000, published in 1998, was sponsored by Group 5, in association with the Electronic Original Initiative.

Introduction

Information communications

Many electronic documents which were created on computer systems will be sent under manual or automatic control to other computer systems. Electronic communications systems that send data (which itself is stored in compliance with Part 1) from one location to another need to be configured and operated in such a manner that the authenticity of the electronic documents is not compromised. Many existing electronic document communications systems are insecure, with the possibility of files being intercepted and amended during the communication process without the knowledge of the sender or the recipient.

The Code seeks to define operational procedures which comply with 'good practice' in the field of electronic document communications. Following its recommendations ensures that the organization implements well controlled and structured systems, with minimum risk of authenticity being challenged, and with minimum risk of security breaches.

Compliance with the Code does not guarantee legal admissibility. It does not follow that electronic documents which are communicated by systems not in compliance with this Code are not legally admissible, but it may be more difficult to prove their integrity in court.

In some cases, where two parties reach prior agreement on a joint communications policy, documents exchanged electronically within this agreement should be acceptable in court or other dispute resolution environment. In this case, legal advice needs to be sought on the wording of the agreement to ensure that the technical details are appropriate. Such agreements may not require compliance with the Code, but to do so would improve their acceptability to a court.

In order to provide widely applicable guidance, the Code does not specify system hardware or software configurations, and thus is technology independent.

Details of the content of a communicated document are not relevant to the Code. Thus, the Code is equally applicable to simple 'message' documents and to complex multi-sectioned (compound) documents. In the Code, all such documents are included under the term 'electronic communication'.

Electronic mail (email), instant messaging (IM), web services, web forms, XML, messages, mobile messaging (SMS), electronic data interchange (EDI) are increasingly being used for business communications. Many of these are 'free format' and give great flexibility of content; Chapter 1 gives guidelines for the development of an organizational policy for the creation, transmission and receipt of these unstructured forms of electronically communicated document.

Purpose of the Code

Users of electronic communications systems are being asked by their companies, government departments and other employers to review the legal issues relevant to their use. The application of these systems is changing the way in which many aspects of business and organizational life are operated, as electronic communications are increasingly replacing the more traditional paper-based methods. Different electronic communications systems and devices have their own inherent advantages and limitations and existing systems will, at some later stage, be replaced or become obsolete. The purpose of the Code is to assist organizations in dealing with the implications, specifically concerning evidential and legal issues, of this technological evolution.

The Code provides a framework and guidelines that identify key areas of good practice for the implementation and operation of such electronic communications systems, whether or not any such information is ever required as evidence in the event of a dispute. As such, compliance with the Code should be regarded as a demonstration of responsible business management.

Management framework

Chapters 1–5 of the Code are structured according to a set of 'Five Principles of Good Practice', defined in PD 0010:1997, *Principles of Good Practice for Information Management*. The Five Principles take the form of a set of statements of objectives for information management. These are intended to act as guidelines for a set of procedures and controls that any organization would be capable of implementing as an extension of their current standard operating procedures, or of their quality management processes. In other cases some of the recommended controls may already exist as part of a set of industry regulations.

Thus, instead of attempting to specify in detail what these procedures need to be, it is understood that different industry sectors will have different procedural requirements. They may need to use the Five Principles only as a checklist to test the conformance to existing regulations of their current processes and procedures and how they meet legal and regulatory requirements. From current experience of several business sectors, however, many organizations will find that they have insufficient or inadequate controls and/or procedures in place. For these organizations, the Five Principles are intended to provide a starting point for the development of their electronic information management and electronic commerce applications.

The main advantage in taking this approach is a set of principles which are device-independent and which should outlive any particular configuration of technology, and thus will still be of value when following generations of software, storage and other devices come into play.

The Five Principles, as defined in PD 0010, are:

1. recognize and understand all types of information;
2. understand the legal issues and execute 'duty of care' responsibilities;
3. identify and specify business processes and procedures;
4. identify enabling technologies to support business processes and procedures;
5. monitor and audit business processes and procedures.

The ordering of the Five Principles also reflects a cascade from the high level classification of information streams to responsibilities, and then on to operational, technological and system monitoring considerations.

These principles are reflected in the Code as follows:

1. information management policy (see Chapter 1);
2. duty of care (see Chapter 2);
3. procedures and processes (see Chapter 3);
4. enabling technologies (see Chapter 4);
5. audit trails (see Chapter 5).

These five chapters, each representing one of the Five Principles of Good Practice, contain details of processes and procedures that need to be put into place to ensure compliance with the Code.

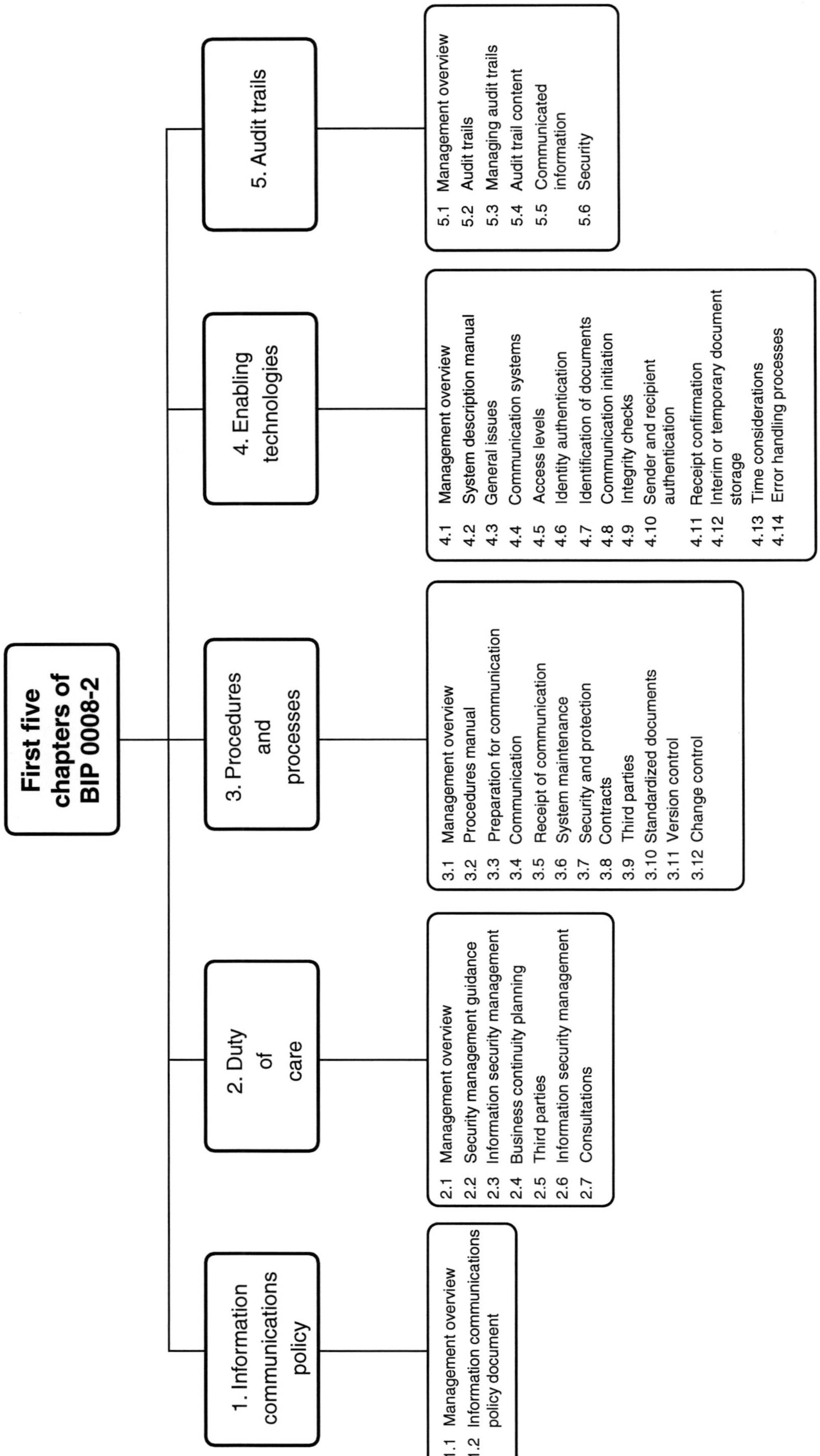
First five chapters of BIP 0008-2
1. Information communications policy
1.1 Management overview
1.2 Information communications policy document
2. Duty of care
2.1 Management overview
2.2 Security management guidance
2.3 Information security management
2.4 Business continuity planning
2.5 Third parties
2.6 Information security management
2.7 Consultations
3. Procedures and processes
3.1 Management overview
3.2 Procedures manual
3.3 Preparation for communication
3.4 Communication
3.5 Receipt of communication
3.6 System maintenance
3.7 Security and protection
3.8 Contracts
3.9 Third parties
3.10 Standardized documents
3.11 Version control
3.12 Change control
4. Enabling technologies
4.1 Management overview
4.2 System description manual
4.3 General issues
4.4 Communication systems
4.5 Access levels
4.6 Identity authentication
4.7 Identification of documents
4.8 Communication initiation
4.9 Integrity checks
4.10 Sender and recipient authentication
4.11 Receipt confirmation
4.12 Interim or temporary document storage
4.13 Time considerations
4.14 Error handling processes
5. Audit trails
5.1 Management overview
5.2 Audit trails
5.3 Managing audit trails
5.4 Audit trail content
5.5 Communicated information
5.6 Security

Plan-Do-Check-Act model

The Plan-Do-Check-Act model, or PDCA for short, has been adopted by a number of management systems standards, such as those for quality management (BS EN ISO 9001:2000), environmental management (BS EN ISO 14001:2004) and information security management [BS ISO/IEC 27001 (BS 7799-2)]. The PDCA model emphasizes how critical it is for effective risk management that an ongoing management process is in place, and is exercised.

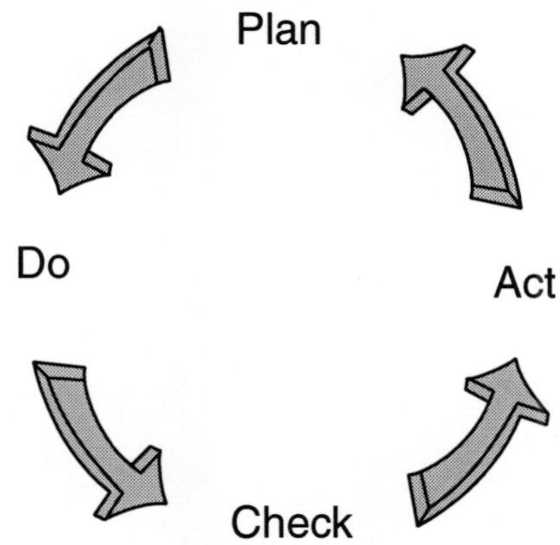

The Code follows a similar approach, with the first five chapters mapped closely to the 'Plan', 'Do' and 'Check' phases of the PDCA model, as shown in the diagram below. This facilitates greater harmonization with the management systems standards (and/or other publications). This is particularly important where an organization is complying with more than one management systems publication, for example the Code and [BS ISO/IEC 27001 (BS 7799-2)], because repetition and overlap can be minimized whilst reducing the likelihood of compliance gaps.

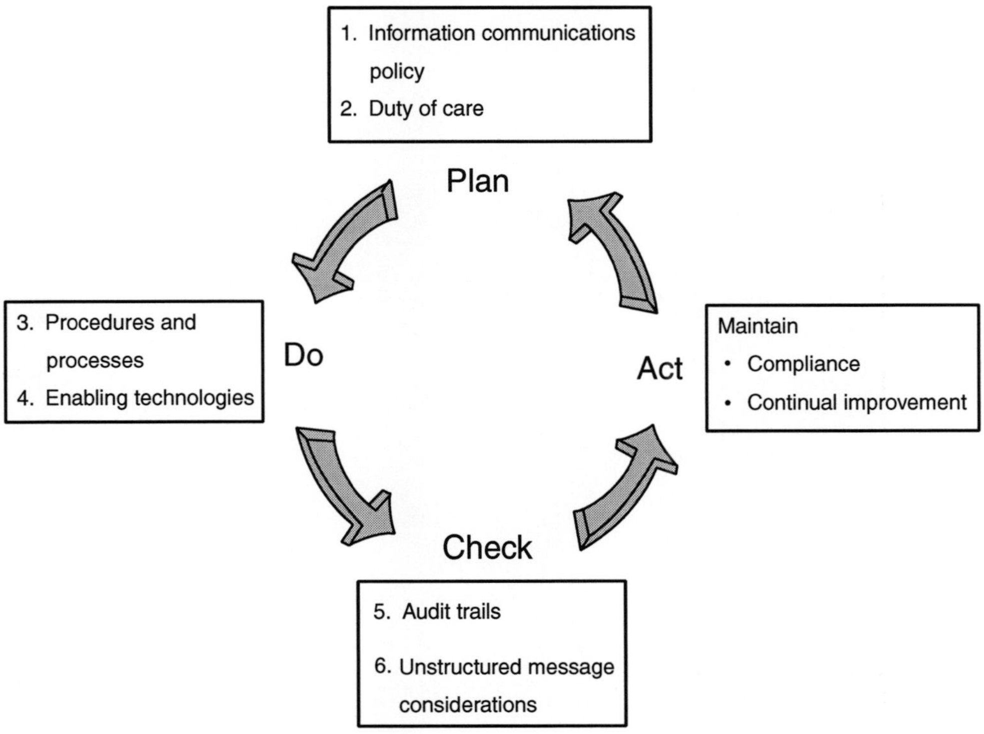

The use of the PDCA model is of particular benefit to the Code, in that it adds emphasis to the importance of feedback and continual improvement within the 'Act' phase.

General

Scope

The Code describes procedures and processes for transferring electronic documents from one computer system to another where the issues of authenticity, integrity and availability as required by legal admissibility and evidential weight of the sent and/or received document are important, typically where two organizations are involved. Whilst specific systems are not addressed by the Code, the requirements of the system (both system and procedural) are included.

> ***Definitions***
>
> **Authenticity – Trustworthiness of origin and evidential content**
>
> **Integrity – Retention of the evidential content of the information**
>
> **Availability – Accessibility of the information as required**

Electronic document communications are being used increasingly for electronic trading, where a 'document' is often described as a 'transaction' or a 'message' (e.g. in e-commerce applications). Such systems can be operated under the requirements of the Code.

The sender and/or recipient of a data file may be a person, an organization, an application or a computer system. In many instances there will be a 1:1 relationship between sender and recipient, the Code applies to these and situations where there are many recipients and a single sender.

The Code is for use with any type of computer file using a wide range of communications infrastructures. Data files may contain binary data, text, image, CAD data, moving or still video images, audio or any combination of these or similar data types or may be computer software files (or any combination).

Applicability

The Code is applicable to communications systems which use computer networks or which use remote data file transmission systems via an electronic communications carrier. It also addresses circuit switched or electronic communication switched systems. The data file transmission may be by telephone circuit, cable, radio or satellite communications technology (or any combination).

As such it can be applied to message-based systems where a complete transaction is built up and sent as a whole to another user (e.g. fax, email, EDI using a VAN, e-business using the internet). It may also be applied where a user is communicating interactively with a remote system and building up a transaction as a set of parts (e.g. web forms).

The users

The Code is intended for:

- end user organizations that wish to ensure that information communicated electronically may be used with confidence as evidence in any dispute, within or outside a court of law;

- integrators and developers of electronic communications systems which provide facilities to meet user requirements.

Objectives

The objectives of the Code are to:

- improve reliability of, and confidence in, communicated information;
- maximize the evidential weight which a court or other body may assign to presented information;
- provide confidence in inter-company trading;
- provide confidence to external inspectors (for example, regulators and auditors) that the organization's information and business communications practices are robust and reliable.

The Code may be used as a common reference standard for business activities within and between organizations and for sub-contracting or procurement of information technology services or products.

Compliance

Each chapter of the Code contains a general description of the issues being addressed, followed by a list of 'key issues'. These indicate the critical compliance points that need to be taken into consideration, and acted upon where appropriate, before compliance with the recommendations of the Code can be claimed. Compliance is claimed on a voluntary basis, by self-certification.

The key issues in this publication will be expanded into questions, and published as the Compliance Workbook (BIP 0009-2). These questions relate to the text in the related chapters in the Code. It is recommended that compliance is claimed only after all relevant questions have been answered positively.

Typical compliance statements are shown in 5.3.7. See also 5.3.6 for information on compliance audits.

Key requirements

Included in the controls for this part of the Code are a number of underlying criteria which, when complied with, provide assurances that electronic communications have been sent and received in a controlled and understandable manner. As such they are applicable to both sender and recipient of the electronic communication.

The key requirements for maximizing the evidential weight of electronic messages are:

Sender authentication	Proving the sender identity (see BIP 0008-3:2005)
Integrity	Ensuring the content of the electronic communication is what it purports to be
Identity	Identifying the electronic communication
Date and time of communication	Identifying the time of communication
Confirmation	Confirming receipt
Date and time of receipt	Identifying the time of delivery and/or collection
Recipient authentication	Proving the recipient identity (see BIP 0008-3:2005)

Trusted third party services

Many current electronic communications systems may fail to provide adequate assurances concerning electronic communication delivery. Delivery of an electronic communication by a trusted third party service provider can, in normal circumstances, provide strong independent evidence of the key requirements detailed in 2.5. As such, use of these facilities can provide equal or greater evidential weight, compared with that provided by an electronic communication not using this facility.

eg

Example

Email has become an essential business tool, but it must be used with care if the sender or recipient is to rely upon email in the event of dispute. It is not technically difficult to make an email appear to come from someone other than the real sender. This ID 'spoofing' is used extensively by spammers to mask their identities. In addition, because of the specifications used by the underlying technologies that make Internet email so powerful and interoperable, there is no guarantee of immediate delivery, or in fact delivery ever. A sender simply requesting an email delivery receipt is not totally reliable as many systems are configured to withhold them; this is frequently to prevent the spammers from using the delivery receipt request to validate email address details.

If you need to rely on sender identity or proof of delivery then additional safeguards need to be taken.

Where the trusted third party service is retaining an archive copy of the message, this should be retained in accordance with Part 1.

Recipient's perspective

From the recipient's perspective, the main areas of challenge are as follows:

1. The sender is not who he purports to be;

2. The electronic communication was not received, or was received multiple times; or,

3. The electronic communication has been changed in some way in transit.

eg

Example

An email may not be delivered at all, or it may be delivered multiple times. For many electronic communications, repeated delivery is merely an inconvenience.

For many electronic transactions, however, it is potentially dangerous:

- **Would you really want to have duplicate payments appearing on your credit card statement?**

- **Does a business want to stop selling a particular product because it believes it is sold out, only to find that one of the apparent sales was, in fact, just a duplicate of a real order?**

> **Such transactions need solid proof of delivery, so that a duplicate communication is rejected and, if a receipt is not received within a predefined time, the message is re-sent.**
>
> **Such proof of delivery is normally a fundamental component of the message queuing technologies that underpin web services and service-oriented architectures.**

Electronic communications communicated in compliance with the terms of this Code will allow the recipient to check sender authentication and electronic communication identity and integrity.

Where a received electronic communication is questionable, procedures that verify its origin and integrity need to be used. Such procedures may include sending the electronic communication back to the supposed sender, with a request for a confirmation of receipt and integrity.

Documentation

Compliance with the Code requires the availability and use of specified documentation. This documentation consists of:

- information communications policy document (see 1.2);
- information security policy document (see 2.3.2);
- procedures manual (see 3.2);
- system description manual (see 4.2).

The availability of these documents, and demonstrable adherence to the procedures described therein, should, if effectively constructed, provide the audit trail that may be used to demonstrate the authenticity of communicated information, and thus enhance its evidential weight.

Note that each of the documents mentioned above may actually be maintained as multiple documents, or these documents may be combined. The key recommendation is that the documentation exists, is maintained, and is readily accessible to those authorized within the organization and to any authorized third party who may require access. It may also be appropriate to use the documents created in accordance with Part 1 of the Code, and extend them to cover the requirements of this part of the Code.

All documentation needs to be maintained in line with existing working practices, and thus should be maintained under a version control system (see 3.11).

Additional documentation may be required to support the daily operation of the system, for example:

- system maintenance log (see 3.6);
- audit trail (see Chapter 5);
- compliance statements (see 5.3.7).

The content of documentation described above can easily become unreliable where there are no procedures in place to ensure that they keep pace with both organizational and system changes. Unreliable documentation may adversely affect legal arguments relating to the correct operation of an information communications system. It is therefore important to ensure that the definitive versions of system documents are brought under configuration management control, and are firmly linked to the organization's change management procedures.

Where compliance with the Code is claimed over a period of time during which different editions of the above documentation were appropriate, then all editions of this documentation should be kept, in compliance with the policy document. This is to ensure that, where information regarding the system at a point in the past is required, it can be obtained from this document store.

Chapter 1 Information communications policy

1.1 Management overview

Increasingly, electronic documents are being sent from one computer system to another, either within an organization or between organizations. The manner in which this movement of information occurs may determine the success or failure of the organization. Thus, communications systems need to be secure, structured and auditable.

Electronic communications systems need to be classified, structured and validated by the organization. Where a document is received electronically from another organization, knowledge of the processes used to communicate the document is key to a successful, legally admissible electronic communications system.

When defining communication policy, the relative importance of speed of delivery, both to the recipient organization and to the recipient in that organization, may be significant. Taking two extremes, direct communication to a PC across the internet or via a carrier usually results in almost instantaneous communication, whereas communication by post may be measured in days.

Part 1 of BIP 0008 requires the classification of all documents used by an organization into 'document types'. This classification leads to the creation of a 'policy document' which should be extended to accommodate the communicated documents covered in this Part of the Code.

1.2 Information communications policy document

1.2.1 Structure

Different types of documents may be communicated within an organization, or between organizations, using different data file transmission systems. To enable implementation of such systems, the organization needs a policy statement that can be used to guide implementers, and to demonstrate to other parties that systems used were in line with policy.

To implement the Code, the policy document produced in compliance with Part 1 should be extended to include policy on electronic communication.

The policy document should be approved by senior management of the organization, and should be reviewed for relevance and content at regular intervals. The frequency for review should be appropriate to the application.

This period will typically be the same as the normal procedural audit cycle within the organization (e.g. annual or in the event of major changes to the system).

There will frequently be more than one type of data file transmission system in use within an organization. The communication requirements for each document type needs to be reviewed, based on timeliness and service levels. Cost may also be a consideration.

In order to align communication requirements with specific electronic documents, a document 'type' designation should be allocated. These 'types' may be described by application (e.g. financial reports, stock lists), or by information content (e.g. invoice, order).

Annex A includes an example policy document, which may be used during the drafting of an organization's policy document. It contains some 'typical' statements that may be appropriate in many policy statements.

The policy should set out guidelines for the appropriate communication channel for each document 'type'.

eg

Example

For some electronic transactions, multiple different communications channels will be offered. These may have different characteristics, each variant of which needs to be considered.

For example a single transaction could be sent by email, voice message, SMS or IM depending on sender or recipient preferences. Similarly, a website could offer a web form to complete, or a downloadable form to be completed and emailed or faxed.

The policy should address the following objectives:

Subject	*Content*	*Section*
Communications	Set guidelines for the communication of specific electronic documents	1.2.2
Compression	Set guidelines for the use of data compression	1.2.3
Encryption	Set guidelines for the use of encryption	1.2.4
Procedures	Set guidelines for procedures to be followed by employees when using communication facilities to send electronic documents	1.2.5
Delivery/receipt	Set policy for procedures to be followed on delivery or receipt of a communicated file	1.2.6
Responsibilities	Define responsibilities for information communication	1.2.7

Comment

A single message may have a different value to the sender and to the recipient. Communication system requirements may thus vary depending upon individual requirements, or a combination of requirements.

Example

Any electronic transaction involves two or more parties, it is quite usual for the significance to be completely different for the different parties. It is, as a result, quite common for the controls and guidelines for a transaction (and its storage under the controls of Part 1 of BIP 0008) to be different for the different parties involved, even when they are within the same organization.

For example, an electronic expenses claim may involve an individual employee, his authorizing manager and the department responsible for payroll. The payroll department may have no first hand knowledge of the employee or the manager and would therefore need independent evidence as to their identities, as linked to the claim (unlike the employee, who knows their manager). Both employee and manager are less concerned over authenticating the identity of the payroll department, they would realize something was amiss when the expenses were not reimbursed with the pay.

Key issue

Develop and have approved by senior management an information communications policy.

Ensure it is reviewed at regular intervals, as appropriate to the application.

1.2.2 Communications

There are many forms of technologies and procedures that can be used for electronic communications. The organization's policy document should set guidelines for appropriate systems to be used for all corporate electronic communications.

In particular, the use of structured and unstructured forms of electronic communications should be included. Where unstructured electronic communications are involved, corporate guidelines on message structures should be included within the policy document, or referenced by it.

> **Key issue**
>
> **The policy document should give guidance on the type of communications technology to use in particular circumstances, and the content and layout of unstructured communications.**

1.2.3 Compression

Some electronic communications will need to be compressed before being communicated. This may be due to:

- a large file size (a smaller, compressed file will require less transmission time);
- a large number of individual files (these can be compressed into a single file);
- the application of a compression key to improve electronic document security.

The policy document should give guidance on when compression is to be used, and how to formulate compression keys.

> **Key issue**
>
> **The policy document should give guidance on the use of compression tools.**

1.2.4 Encryption

Encryption can be used to improve the security of electronic communications, by the addition of encryption keys. Access to encrypted electronic documents can only be achieved by the application of the appropriate decryption key.

The policy document should state the organization's policy on when encryption is to be used, and how to formulate encryption keys. It should also include policy on the security and access arrangements appropriate to encryption keys.

> **Key issue**
>
> **The policy document should give guidance on the use of encryption technology.**

1.2.5 Procedures

The policy document should provide guidelines on the requirement for appropriate procedures to be followed when electronic communications are being undertaken. Details of these procedures can be found in Chapter 3. These procedures may need to link to the corporate information security policy as detailed in 2.3.

> ***Key issue***
>
> **The policy document should give guidelines on procedures necessary to use corporate electronic communications systems.**

1.2.6 Delivery/receipt

In relation to the Code, the critical procedural issues are related to the delivery of and the receipt of electronic communications. Thus, the policy document should give guidelines on how these procedures are developed, and to what standards. These procedures include:

- avoidance of messages with illegal content;
- avoidance of copyright issues;
- protection against malicious software;
- appropriate security procedures;
- application of corporate retention policies;
- avoidance of spam and similar messages (incoming and outgoing).

> ***Key issue***
>
> **The policy document should give guidelines on the procedures required to protect the organization, where electronic communications are sent and/or received.**

1.2.7 Responsibility

The policy document should include a statement, for each document type being communicated, of the party responsible for the information.

This party may be a person, a job function or a computer application controlled by a person.

> ***Key issue***
>
> **Identify individual responsibilities for information communications.**
>
> **Detail these in the policy document.**

Chapter 2 Duty of care

2.1 Management overview

It is essential that an organization is aware of the value of information that is communicated within the organization, or with its trading partners. This awareness includes an understanding of 'duty of care' principles.

The implications of an insecure electronic communications system may be far reaching, and potentially damaging to an organization. In order to ensure the integrity of electronic information prior to, or after communication, they need to be stored under the controls in Part 1 of BIP 0008. If, however, electronic information stored in compliance with Part 1 is communicated by a system not in compliance with the Code, its legal admissibility may be compromised.

Suitable guidelines, which specify system security requirements, may already exist in organizational policies or working practices. There may also be sector-specific guidance (e.g. financial, pharmaceutical), national or international standards, or legal requirements. Where these do not exist, suitable guidelines need to be developed, approved and implemented.

Security guidelines for electronic communications should be devised and implemented, as appropriate to the organization concerned. These security guidelines should be applied to electronic communications systems.

2.2 Security management guidance

Publications are available which provide advice in devising comprehensive sets of information security guidelines to meet the organization's needs.[1] These guidelines should be included in the organization's review process. For some applications, the adoption of externally accredited security schemes as additional confirmation of compliance to their security policy may be appropriate.

There are a number of National and International Standards that, if implemented, should support the organization's demonstration of duty of care (see next comment box). Standards which cover information security and service quality issues are particularly appropriate.

---

[1] See the BIP 0070 series on information security management (previously the PD 3000 series).

Comment

The internationally accepted information security management standards are:

1 BS ISO/IEC 17799 (BS 7799-1), *Information technology — Security techniques — Code of practice for information security management*;

2 BS ISO/IEC 27001 (BS 7799-2), *Information technology — Security techniques — Information security management systems — Requirements*.

Information is the lifeblood of all organizations and can exist in many forms. It can be stored electronically and transmitted by mail or by electronic means. In the competitive business environment, such information is constantly under threat from many sources. These can be internal, external, accidental, or malicious.

These information security management standards address these issues and have thus been implemented in many major organizations. They are referenced in many places and are becoming the common benchmark against which information security is measured.

Within the UK, there is a formal certification scheme against the requirements of BS ISO/IEC 27001 (BS 7799-2). A number of UK and overseas organizations have seen the benefit of compliance, particularly where they offer IT services to other organizations. Other organizations have used the two documents to assess their information security management systems, as part of their risk assessment processes.

It is important that any decisions made concerning certification or compliance with the standards are recorded by the organization.

Key issue

Where an appropriate National or International Standard is implemented, electronic communications systems should be included with the scope of compliance with the Standard.

2.3 Information security management

2.3.1 Security elements

To fulfil the duty of care objective, the organization needs to action the following:

Subject	*Action*	*Section*
Policy	Implement an information security policy	2.3.2
Risk	Carry out a risk assessment and implement appropriate recommendations	2.3.3
Infrastructure	Develop, implement and test an information security management system	2.3.4
Business continuity	Develop, implement and test a business continuity plan	2.4
Third parties	Develop policies and procedures for working with third parties	2.5
Information security	Where appropriate, use BS ISO/IEC 17799 (BS 7799-1)	2.6
Consultations	Identify who needs to be consulted, to ensure legal, regulatory and business compliance	2.7

2.3.2 Information security policy

All information that is in the process of electronic communications is vulnerable to loss or change, whether accidental or malicious. To protect such information, appropriate security measures need to be implemented to reduce the risk of a successful challenge to its authenticity or integrity.

Information security, whether in the area of confidentiality, integrity or availability (see 2.6.1), is not simply a constraint to be placed upon computer systems. Security and access to the physical environment (e.g. buildings, networks, etc.) and the implementation of policies and procedures by all staff are key elements.

The organization should adopt an information security policy for electronic communications (sending and/or receiving as appropriate).

Where the organization has an information security policy for other processes (for example storage), then it should be extended to incorporate the requirements of the electronic communications system within its scope.

The information security policy document should contain (for the electronic communications systems), as a minimum:

- the scope of the information security policy;
- a statement of the management objectives regarding information security for electronic communications (sending and/or receiving as appropriate);
- specific policy statements;
- requirements for different information classification categories;

- definition and allocation of electronic communications responsibilities;
- electronic communications training and awareness requirements;
- policy for dealing with potential or actual compromise of electronic communications systems;
- policy regarding compliance with appropriate Standards;
- approval and review process.

The information security policy should be approved by the organization's senior management. The organization should then agree and document appropriate levels of security for managing its information communications systems, in compliance with its stated information security policy.

Key issue

Develop, authorize and implement an information security policy.

Ensure that the policy's scope includes the information communications systems.

2.3.3 Risk assessment

Information security measures are often applied piecemeal, reacting to security incidents or to available computer software tools. This type of approach can fail to recognize the value of the information asset and the risks to the organization from security compromise during electronic communication. This may leave gaps in security, which may be filled only at some later date after a security breach.

A more structured approach is to review the information assets and assign risk factors (based on asset value, system vulnerability and likelihood of attack). The security policy can then be produced and approved against the value model.

The organization should undertake an information security risk assessment aligned to the electronic communications systems, and record the results.

Existing security measures should be reviewed for effectiveness. Factors such as the balance between the cost of implementation and the security achieved should be taken into consideration during the review process.

Where different types of electronic communications systems can be used, their individual impact on the risk assessment results should be reviewed.

Key issue

Perform a risk assessment of existing security measures, and implement cost-effective technology and/or procedures to fill any gaps found.

2.3.4 Information security infrastructure

In order to control and manage security issues with electronic communications systems, a management infrastructure needs to be implemented, including relevant electronic communications systems within its scope. The infrastructure should have as its objectives:

- approval and review of the information security policy;
- monitoring of threats to information security;
- monitoring and review of security breaches;
- approval of major initiatives to enhance information security.

> ***Key issue***
>
> **Plan and implement an information security framework.**

2.4 Business continuity planning

The unavailability of electronic communications systems (even for a matter of minutes in some applications) can be a serious problem for organizations. Thus, procedures are required which need to be implemented, to control and minimize the impact of such a situation.

There is also the issue of recovery from failure during a particular communication. It is important to ensure that transmission occurs once and only once, even when a transmission is interrupted by system failure (see also 3.5.6).

> ***Example***
>
> **If a company's website is unavailable, even for a few minutes, valuable orders may be lost. Similarly, if the EDI service that is such an integral part of the 'just in time' supply chain is out of service, the order for parts might be delayed and production halted because of their shortfall.**
>
> **These are very clear and direct results from a loss of service without adequate and effective business continuity plans being in place; the unavailability of a system such as email can be less obvious, but just as damaging for the business. Deprived of the main communications channel that is email, how many knowledge workers quickly cease to function effectively? To get the picture, just look at the crowd that forms around the drinks machine if the email server is down!**

Business continuity for electronic communications systems is not managed simply by the availability of suitable alternative communications facilities, as the unavailability of premises, staff or hardware needs to be included. Such procedures may involve the temporary use of additional or third party resources.

In order to ensure that the integrity and availability of information is not compromised during electronic communications, an agreed and approved business continuity plan should be implemented, covering the electronic communications systems.

eg

Example

A key aspect to consider when developing and testing a business continuity plan is how long it takes to get a failed system back into full operation.

With an email service, it is not simply a case of getting the mail server back online, which may only take a matter of minutes. Without access to the contents of inbox, sent items, shared and personal folders, contact lists, calendar and diary, the email users will, quite rightly, perceive that the email system is inadequate. Recovery of all these components may take hours longer than simply restarting the mail server.

Procedures should be established to include:

- major equipment, environmental or personnel failure;
- testing such procedures;
- maintaining such procedures;
- ensuring such procedures do not compromise the integrity of information during their implementation;
- ensuring such procedures do not result in unwitting loss of electronically communicated documents.

eg

Example

Many electronic communications systems include automated retry processes where successful transmission has not been completed.

With fax, there are standards governing how many times and how frequently a failed transmission may be retried automatically (but note that some low facility fax machines do not support this feature at all); these standards were originally set to restrict the number of 'annoyance' calls when a wrong number was entered into the sending fax.

With Internet email, the SMTP (Simple Mail Transfer Protocol) process will automatically re-try a transfer if, for example, the recipients mail server is offline. In many cases the sender is totally unaware that this has happened. When repeated SMTP retries are required, the time before a subsequent retry is extended and may quickly become measured in days rather than minutes or hours.

Key issue

Business continuity plans should include procedures which ensure the integrity of communicated information and, in particular, information in the process of being communicated at the time of failure.

2.5 Third parties

All information that is being communicated via a third party is potentially vulnerable to loss or change, whether accidental or malicious. To protect such information, appropriate security measures need to be implemented to minimize the risk of such a loss or change, and thus a successful challenge to its authenticity.

Where the third party is retaining communicated information for a period, however short, they should have adopted an information security policy in relation to this information. This policy may need to be incorporated within or referred to by the organization's own information security policy; this means the third party will be formally 'trusted'.

Where the trusted third party has an information security policy for other processes (for example storage), the use of the electronic communication should be incorporated within its scope.

Example

One area that trusted third parties will frequently have covered in their security policy is that electronic communications with them should be over secure, encrypted channels. This will prevent eavesdropping on the message and will allow them to authenticate the identity of the person or system accessing their systems. This will frequently use either SSL or TLS.

Such use of a secure channel is also often used for secure mail applications or access to webmail services. A number of secure email services are based on the approach of sending, using a normal email service, a link to a message held on a secure web server. The recipient follows the link using their browser and will only be able to access the confidential message over an SSL or TLS protected channel which will only be opened up to them when they have successfully identified themselves as the intended recipient. Note though that such secure channels may mean that information is not checked by the organization's boundary defences intended to prevent access to inappropriate or dangerous material.

Definition – SSL and TLS

SSL is short for Secure Sockets Layer, a protocol for confidential transmission across the Internet. SSL works by using a private key to encrypt data that is transferred over the SSL connection. Most browsers support SSL and many websites use the protocol to obtain confidential user information, like credit card numbers. Normally, URLs that require an SSL connection start with https: instead of http:.

Another protocol for transmitting data securely over the World Wide Web is Secure HTTP (S-HTTP).

SSL creates a secure channel connection between a client and a server, over which any amount of data can be sent securely. S-HTTP is designed to transmit individual messages securely. SSL and S-HTTP are therefore complementary rather than competing. Both protocols are standards approved by the Internet Engineering Task Force (IETF).

SSL is being superseded by TLS (Transport Layer Security) and is an extension of SSL. TLS is a newer protocol for privacy and data integrity between client/server applications communicating over the Internet.

The TLS protocol is made up of two layers:

- **The TLS Record Protocol – ensures that the connection is private by using symmetric data encryption and it ensures that the connection is reliable. The TLS Record Protocol is also used for encapsulation of higher-level protocols, such as the TLS Handshake Protocol;**
- **The TLS Handshake Protocol – allows authentication between the server and client and the negotiation of an encryption algorithm and cryptographic keys before the application protocol transmits or receives any data.**

TLS and SSL are not interoperable.

Where a third party provides communication services (for example where a value added network provider manages EDI systems), such services should be included within the scope of compliance with the Code. Services should include appropriate recovery and disaster recovery processes.

The provider of third party services needs to be aware of the value of the service that it provides, and needs to execute its responsibility under the 'duty of care' principle.

To fulfil this objective, the provider of third party services should ensure that they:

- are aware of legislation and regulatory bodies pertinent to themselves and their client's industry sector;

- are aware of legislation pertinent to countries (or other geographical areas) where their services are delivered;
- establish a chain of accountability and assign responsibility for activities involving communications services at all levels;
- keep abreast of developments by keeping in contact with the appropriate bodies and organizations;
- be aware of any legislative or regulatory control of trusted third party services.

Similarly and reciprocally, the organization should ensure that the third party:

- is aware of legislation and regulatory bodies pertinent to the trusted third party's industry;
- is aware of legislation pertinent to countries (or other geographical areas) where its services are delivered;
- establishes a chain of accountability and assigns responsibility for activities involving communications services at all levels;
- keeps abreast of developments by keeping in contact with the appropriate bodies and organizations;
- is aware of any legislative or regulatory control of trusted third party services.

Where appropriate, organizations should request documentation which demonstrates the third party's duty of care, as part of the agreed contract.

> ***Key issue***
>
> **When communications systems use third party resources, the third party should only be considered to be 'trusted' where they have an appropriate information security policy.**
>
> **Where a third party provides communications services, such services should be included in the organization's information security policy.**

2.6 Information security principles

2.6.1 General

BS ISO/IEC 17799 (BS 7799-1) is the UK reference document for information security management. Proof of compliance with the recommendations of this Standard, when implemented within the boundaries covered by the Code, may provide helpful supporting evidence in court. It will indicate that the organization has exercised its duty of care, and it will assist the court in assessing the authenticity and integrity of the information.

BS ISO/IEC 27001 (BS 7799-2) is an auditable specification for use in the certification of an information security management system against the Standard.

Compliance with the requirements of BS ISO/IEC 17799 9 (BS 7799-1) or certification against BS ISO/IEC 27001 (BS 7799-2) should not be regarded as an alternative to compliance with the recommendations of this Code.

BS ISO/IEC 17799 (BS 7799-1) includes details of an information security model, classifying information security into three areas (the 'CIA' principle):

- Confidentiality;
- Integrity;
- Availability.

The relevance of all three of these principles should be reviewed and suitable procedures and processes implemented.

2.6.2 Confidentiality

Where appropriate, data being communicated should be protected from unauthorized access.

> ***Comment***
>
> **Confidentiality is about protecting data from unauthorized access. Historically, information security has been thought of as confidentiality, ensuring that information is not available outside the intended authorized group. Whilst this is important and in some cases critical to the organization, it is not the most important security issue relevant to this part of the Code.**

> ***Key issue***
>
> **Ensuring confidentiality in electronic communications should be as appropriate to business needs. Confidentiality is not an important requirement of the Code.**

2.6.3 Integrity

Integrity is about ensuring that the content of a data file is what it purports to be. Thus, it is key to the achievement of legal admissibility, as it is about ensuring data accuracy and completeness. When considering security, it is necessary to assess the risk of integrity being compromised and compare with the cost of protection against such compromise. Security measures may include the application of encryption technology to reduce the risk of changes to information.

Procedures and processes should be implemented to ensure the integrity of electronic documents during communication. Some systems use file names linked to MAC codes or digital signatures for this purpose (see 3.5.6).

Data recovery procedures, to be implemented in the case of failure of the electronic document communications system, should be such as to maintain the integrity of the relevant data.

> ***Key issue***
>
> **Ensuring integrity is the key issue to legal admissibility. Processes and procedures should be adopted in relation to the value to the organization of the information being communicated.**

2.6.4 Availability

Availability is about ensuring that the data is available when it is required by an authorized user. Loss of data could be interpreted as being just as significant as fraudulent modification. It may be necessary to demonstrate that specific information is still available for a legally stipulated time after communication. In this area, topics such as regular backup and business continuity planning are critical. These topics are dealt with in Part 1 of BIP 0008.

Procedures and processes should be implemented which ensure that the electronic document is available as required. This is best implemented by storing documents electronically communicated in compliance with Part 1 of BIP 0008.

> ***Key issue***
>
> **Ensuring that information is available when required is a key requirement.**

2.7 Consultations

There may be international, national and/or regional laws and/or regulations covering the communication of information within, across, into or out of a country. It is thus essential to consult with relevant bodies to ensure the legality of communications systems implemented.

In some countries, it is illegal to communicate particular types of electronic documents. Organizational policies need to identify such documents, and ensure that they are not communicated. Examples of such documents are those which contain obscenities or libellous statements or are encrypted to levels beyond those allowed.

The results of all consultations should be documented and retained in accordance with Part 1 of BIP 0008.

> ***Key issue***
>
> **Relevant bodies should be consulted to ensure the legality of communications systems implemented.**
>
> **The legality of communications (including compression and encryption techniques) of particular types of electronic documents should be determined, and any requirement adhered to.**

Chapter 3 Procedures and processes

3.1 Management overview

This chapter deals with the procedures and processes (automated where appropriate) that need to be implemented as part of an electronic communications system. This will enable the demonstration to internal or external parties that procedures and processes which conformed to the Code were in operation at the appropriate times. The actual procedures implemented are documented in a procedures manual.

3.2 Procedures manual

3.2.1 Documentation

The organization should maintain a procedures manual, which should document (or reference) procedures used for operating the electronic communications system, to ensure its conformity with the controls detailed in the Code.

Where an organization operates a quality management system, such as ISO 9000, then the procedures manual should be included within the quality system.

> *Key issue*
>
> **A procedures manual should be made available, containing details of (or reference to) other relevant documentation concerning all procedures relevant to the information management system.**

3.2.2 Content

The procedures manual should include the topics listed below:

Subject	*Action*	*Section*
Preparation	Ensuring the appropriate documents are prepared for communications	3.3
Communication	Communicating the electronic documents	3.4
Receipt	Capturing the information received	3.5
System maintenance	Physical equipment maintenance	3.6
Security	Complying with the information security policy	3.7
Contracts	Managing the exchange of contracts	3.8
Third parties	Working with third party systems	3.9
Standardized documents Using	templates and other skeleton documents	3.10
Version control	Management of multiple versions of a document	3.11

3.2.3 Compliance with procedures

In order to be able to comply with the procedures detailed in the procedures manual, staff need to be aware of, and have the ability to follow them. This is frequently achieved by training, either by specific courses or during day-to-day working.

> ***Key issue***
>
> **Methods such as training are needed to ensure that all staff who have access to the information management system adhere to agreed procedures.**

3.2.4 Updating and reviews

It is important to ensure that the procedures implemented at any time during the storage life of any specific piece of information can be determined. This is achieved by ensuring that the procedures manual is kept up to date, and that all previous versions are kept in compliance with the policy document (see 1.2).

> ***Key issue***
>
> **All changes to operational procedures should be managed by a change control procedure, to include updating the procedures manual.**
>
> **Current and superseded versions of the procedures manual should be kept in compliance with Part 1 of BIP 0008.**
>
> **The procedures manual should be regularly reviewed, to ensure that it is up to date.**
>
> **All changes should be reviewed to ensure that compliance with the Code is not compromised.**

3.3 Preparation for communication

3.3.1 General

The procedures described in this section are those that should be followed by the sender of an electronic communication.

Procedures used to prepare electronic documents for communication should be documented. Such procedures may be used for example to increase integrity, confidentiality and authenticity, and/or speed of communication.

Where several communication techniques are employed, particular attention should be paid to ensure that the required technique is used in accordance with the policy document.

The use of industry standard software should be considered in all cases, to reduce the risk of file corruption and irretrievability of the communicated information.

3.3.2 Malicious software

Malicious software, such as viruses, macro viruses, worms, Trojan horses, etc., are a major hazard to electronic communications (see also 3.5.2).

Comment

Malware (such as viruses, Trojan horses, worms, etc.) can wreak havoc on information stored in computer systems and on the integrity of information communicated between systems; it can also change the behaviour of previously well-controlled and understood communications systems. It may also prevent such systems from operating at all.

The cost of protection against and recovery from malware can be significant, but the effect of having no protection can be disastrous.

You should warn the organizations with whom you communicate that it is their responsibility to check for viruses, etc.; but if they become aware that you have not had reasonable preventive measures implemented effectively then they may, justifiably, regard your organization as liable for the costs of damage recovery; at the very least they may terminate a trading agreement or generate reputationally damaging adverse publicity for your organization.

Procedures which reduce the possibility of computer viruses and other malicious software being included within information to be communicated should be documented.

Key issue

To protect from the transmission of malicious software, appropriate protection should be installed on the communications systems, and kept up to date.

3.3.3 File compression

File compression may be used to reduce the size of a data file, and thus reduce communication and/or storage costs. Compression may be applied at the time of preparation, or when electronic communication is actioned. The type of compression is usually application-dependent, and may not be under the control of the user.

In a number of environments, the communications channel will compress a file whilst it is in transit; this being transparent to the sender and recipient and implemented to give an improvement in the effective bandwidth of the communications channel.

eg

Example

This type of 'on the wire' compression is most frequently required when slow, costly, transmission links are used. Whilst the sender and recipient may have no choice about this compression being used, they may be well aware of the effect of it.

An example of this is the, now widespread, use of videophones by reporters in the world's troublespots; the lower quality of the video and audio report is deemed an acceptable trade-off for the immediacy of the report.

Another, less obvious, but widespread application of such compression is found with all fax transmissions. In the first part of the communications connection, before the fax image is transferred, the sending and receiving faxes mutually agree the speed of transfer, the resolution of the scanned or otherwise rasterized image, and the compression mechanism for that image, that are supported by both sending and receiving fax systems; this is known as the negotiation phase.

File compression techniques should be used only in accordance with the policy document.

Authenticity should be protected when file compression techniques are implemented.

Where it is important that no information is lost during the compression processes, lossless compression techniques should be used.

Details of the type of compression used (including the lossless/lossy attribute) should be available to the recipient of a compressed data file, if they are required to access the information in that data file and confirm its authenticity.

Compression details may be stored within the data file, within its name (i.e. as the file extension) or as separate metadata. For example, a compression format frequently used for image files is known as 'TIFF'. In this format, the compression method is automatically stored within the file.

Where techniques that are inherently prone to data loss ('lossy') are used, they should be reviewed for acceptability.

eg

Example

Many electronically communicated transactions involve lossy compression. The recipient may be unaware of this, the sender has probably considered it as a key part of the underlying cost model for the transaction.

Most music downloaded from the internet is highly compressed in MP3 or AAC format, giving approximately six or seven times more music than equivalent CD. Interestingly, these same download sites often give an option to receive in the same quality as CD using 'loss-less' compression that is only twice the density of the CD.

Similarly, moving and still images delivered to low memory mobile devices (videophones, PDAs, etc.) will be using lossy compression at different compression rates compared with the same image when downloaded to a PC with its massive hard disk; the MPEG and JPEG compression standards (see PD 0006:1995) for moving and still images respectively are lossy algorithms.

Lossy compression techniques may be acceptable when applied to continuous tone material, grey scale or coloured documents, where loss of information in the scanned image can be shown to be insignificant. Where text or line drawings are involved, however, such techniques may be unacceptable.

Where lossy compression is used, its attributes should be documented. This may be achieved by the use of typical communication files, stored before and after compression.

Key issue

Care should be taken when using lossy compression techniques, as significant information may be lost after decompression. Thus, the resultant document may differ from the original in information content, which may reduce its evidential weight.

3.3.4 File encryption

Where the confidentiality and integrity of information during electronic communications is important, encryption techniques may be used. The information content of data files that are encrypted may not be viewed without the use of a decryption key.

In some applications, 'unprotected' electronic communications pose no threat or risk, where the viewing of information in a communicated file by another party may be acceptable. For such situations encryption may be unnecessary. Other cryptographic techniques, such as digital signatures,[2] however, may be useful in protecting the integrity of the electronic document.

[2] See definition in Part 1 of BIP 0008.

Comment – digital signatures

A digital signature is computed using a set of rules and a set of parameters such that the identity of the signatory and the integrity of the data to which it is applied can be verified. The algorithm used by the digital signature provides the capability to generate and verify signatures. Signature generation systems make use of a private key to generate a digital signature. Signature verification makes use of a public key which corresponds to, but is not the same as, the private key. Each user possesses a private and public key pair. Public keys are assumed to be known to the public in general. Private keys are never shared. Anyone can verify the signature of a user by employing that user's public key. Signature generation can be performed only by the possessor of the user's private key.

A hash function is used in the signature generation process to obtain a condensed version of data, called a message digest. The message digest is then used to generate the digital signature which is sent to the intended verifier along with the signed data (the message). The verifier of the message and signature verifies the signature by using the sender's public key. The same hash function must also be used in the verification process. Similar procedures may be used to generate and verify signatures for stored as well as transmitted data.

The policy document should detail required levels of confidentiality required during communication, for each document type.

Comment

In some circumstances, any requirement for confidentiality may apply only when the data file is being communicated. In this case, encryption of the communications channel as opposed to the data file may be acceptable. With 'channel' encryption, the connection 'pipe' is encrypted along with everything passing over it (and hence anyone eavesdropping), but the contents are 'unprotected' to the communicating parties.

Where 'channel' encryption by itself is insufficient, data file encryption may be appropriate (not necessarily in isolation). Typically this will be necessary where the confidentiality of the data file is required within the sending or receiving system; for example, where only specific individuals are able to see the full text of the document.

eg

Example

Many secure email services utilize S/MIME (Secure/Multipurpose Internet Mail Extensions) which provides a consistent way to send and receive secure MIME data (Internet Engineering Task Force (IETF) RFC 3851). Based on the widely adopted Internet MIME standard, S/MIME provides the following cryptographic security services for electronic messaging applications:

- **Authentication;**
- **message integrity and non-repudiation of origin (using digital signatures); and**
- **data confidentiality (using encryption).**

S/MIME can be used to add cryptographic security services to email that is sent, and to interpret cryptographic security services in received email. However, S/MIME is not restricted to mail; it can be used with any transport mechanism that transports MIME data, such as HTTP. As such, S/MIME takes advantage of the object-based features of MIME and allows secure messages to be exchanged in mixed transport systems.

A note of caution: to enable the internet mail infrastructure to route confidential messages that include S/MIME there are parts of the message that cannot be encrypted, for instance the recipient and sender details. If the fact that these components are 'in clear' is a security risk then the use of an encrypted channel (using SSL or TLS) should be considered.

File encryption techniques should be in accordance with legal requirements of the sender and receiver's jurisdictions, and of any other jurisdiction that the data file passes through (see 2.7).

File encryption techniques should be such that information is not lost during the encryption/decryption processes.

Details of the type of encryption used, and the relevant decryption keys should be available to the recipient if they are required to access the information in the data file.

Where encryption techniques are used, encryption and decryption keys should be stored securely, and be available only to those authorized.

Comment

Legislation may exist mandating, under certain circumstances, disclosure of message content.

An example of this in England and Wales is the Regulation of Investigatory Powers Act 2000, which 'introduces a power to enable properly authorised persons (such as members of the law enforcement, security and intelligence agencies) to serve notices on individuals or bodies requiring the disclosure of protected (e.g. encrypted) information which they lawfully hold, or are likely to, in an intelligible form.' (Explanatory Notes referring to Section 49 of the Act.) Furthermore, the Act also covers disclosure of encryption keys used when messages are sent in encrypted form.

The disclosure of the encrypted message and the keys may be a necessity to establish that the 'intelligible form' was, in fact, the actual encrypted message transmitted.

Procedures for the management and allocation of encryption and decryption keys should be documented. These procedures should include key revocation, key recovery and key escrow processes where appropriate. These procedures are particularly important to cover the situation where the person who was responsible for their management is no longer employed within the organization.

Some countries have laws covering the use of encrypted data files within their jurisdictions. Such requirements should be reviewed and complied with.

Care needs to be exercised where encryption technology is used for the maintenance of the integrity of an electronic document, to ensure that no specific confidentiality-related legislation compliance is compromised.

Example

XML is a major enabler of what the Internet and web services require in order to continue growing and developing as an environment for trustworthy electronic transactions. A lot of work remains to be done on security-related issues before the full capabilities of XML languages are realized. At present, the most important sets of developing specifications in the area of XML-related security are XML encryption, XML signature, XACL, SAML, and XKMS.

Encrypting a complete XML document, testing its integrity, and confirming the authenticity of its sender is a straightforward process. But it is becoming increasingly necessary to use these functions on specific parts of documents rather than the complete XML document, to encrypt and authenticate in arbitrary sequences, and to involve different users or originators.

This may mean, for example, that parts of an XML document are 'in clear' whilst those parts that contain personal data are encrypted.

> ***Key issue***
>
> **File encryption may be used to increase the security on a data file, by reducing the risk of a third party being able to access the information.**

3.3.5 Sender identity

Information may need to be added to an electronic document prior to communication in order to enable the recipient to identify and verify who (individual and/or organization, process, application, system) is the sender of the data file, this is covered in more detail in Part 3 of BIP 0008. Similar identity considerations apply to the identity of the recipient.

> ***Key issue***
>
> **Details of identity information used should be available to the recipient if they are required to verify the identity of the sender of the data file.**

3.3.6 Integrity information

Information may need to be added to a data file prior to electronic communication in order to confirm its integrity. For example see 3.5.6 for details of digital signatures or MAC codes linked to file names.

Where multiple files are being communicated, it may be appropriate to use sequence numbers within file names. These numbers are then used as a completeness check after receipt.

> ***Key issue***
>
> **Details of the integrity confirmation information used should be available to the recipient if they are required to confirm the integrity of the data file.**

3.3.7 Data file format exchange

Information may need to be added to an electronic document prior to communication in order to ensure that the recipient can determine the electronic format of the information content. Details of this format information used should be available to the recipient if they are required to access the information in the data file.

The sender should ascertain the willingness of the recipient to accept a specific data file format. If the recipient indicates that they are unwilling to accept a specific data file format, the sender should select an appropriate, agreed alternative.

Comment– XML

Extensible Markup Language (XML) is a simple, very flexible text format derived from SGML (ISO 8879:1986). Originally designed to meet the challenges of large-scale electronic publishing, XML is also playing an increasingly important role in the exchange of a wide variety of data on the web and elsewhere. The specification of XML is controlled by the World Wide Web Consortium.[3]

XML schemas express shared vocabularies and allow machines to carry out rules made by people. They provide a means for defining the structure, content and semantics of XML documents.

The UK e-Government Interoperability Framework (e-GIF) defines the technical policies and specifications governing information flows across government and the public sector. It covers interconnectivity, data integration, e-services access and content management. Many government processes involve interchange of data, underpinning these transactions are common data definitions within the e-GIF, which are defined as XML schemas for use throughout the public sector.

Another major source of XML schemas is ebXML (Electronic Business using eXtensible Markup Language). It is a modular suite of specifications designed to enable enterprises of any size and in any geographical location to conduct business over the Internet. Using ebXML, companies have a standardized method to exchange business messages, conduct trading relationships, communicate data in common terms and to define and register business processes.

Another useful source of information on the use of XML can be found on the XML website.[4]

Key issue

The acceptance of an agreed format for data file exchange should be documented.

3.3.8 Storage

The electronic document that is to be communicated should be stored in accordance with Part 1 of BIP 0008, along with any associated metadata (e.g. agreed data file format, unique electronic communication identity, time and date stamp, sender and intended recipient identity and address, digital signatures, certificates).

The sender also should subsequently store any receipt confirmation information in accordance with Part 1 of BIP 0008, associated with the communicated document.

Similarly the recipient should store the received communications in accordance with Part 1 of BIP 0008.

[3] Details are to be found at www.w3.org/xml/

[4] www.xml.org

> ***Example***
>
> **The retention requirements of the sender and the recipient of a message may be completely different. This is because the value of the transaction may be completely different to each. For example, the message confirming the receipt of an order of a car is a commonplace event for the motor dealer, but not for the purchaser.**

> ***Key issue***
>
> **Electronic storage should be in compliance with BIP 0008-1:2004.**

3.3.9 Destruction

The procedures implemented by third party service providers (including trusted third parties) when retained information is to be destroyed, deleted or expunged should be documented.

These procedures should be agreed with the organization to ensure that no information that should be retained is inadvertently destroyed, and also to ensure that all information that should be destroyed is not inadvertently retained.

> ***Example***
>
> **Retention requirements are more fully covered in Part 1 of BIP 0008. There are particular cases where communication transaction information has to be retained that is not defined by the business requirements of the business organization or the trusted third party.**
>
> **An example of this is in the requirement for the retention of data by communications service providers ('CSPs') under the terms of the Anti-terrorism, Crime and Security Act 2001 and the subsequent disclosure of such data by CSPs under the terms of the Regulation of Investigatory Powers Act 2000 ('RIPA').**
>
> **The debate about who should fund this retention of data when it is not necessary to be kept for business purposes has been considerable.**

> ***Key issue***
>
> **Where destruction of retained information is required, procedures should be as covered in BIP 0008-1:2004.**

3.3.10 Transfers to archives

Procedures that should be followed when preparing data files for archiving should be documented. This documentation should include details of procedures carried out within the organization or at a third party archive service provider. This documentation should include procedures for identification of data files to be transferred to the archive.

Procedures for preparing for such a transfer (which may be automatic) should be documented. This documentation should include procedures for naming conventions of data files to be transferred to the archive. These conventions should be defined to enable unambiguous subsequent retrieval that may be many years later. Such naming may, by necessity involve date/time, in which case consideration should be given to the uniqueness of such (e.g. time zones, daylight saving time, etc.).

The documentation should include the following procedures for file transfers to the archive:

1. version control of data files – care needs to be taken when a document with the same historical base has been modified or approved by different parties, or at different times;
2. anti-virus controls on data files;
3. approved file formats of data files – where procedures vary depending upon the data file format, each procedure should be documented, together with a procedure which ensures that the correct procedure has been implemented;
4. retention periods of data files – this should clearly differentiate between retention and destruction requirements.

The documentation should also include procedures for the use of the following with data files to be transferred to the archive:

1. encryption and/or compression;
2. digital signatures or other authentication processes.

Key issue

Electronic transfer of documents to archives should be performed in a controlled manner, taking into account any longevity issues such as long-term format accessibility issues.

3.4 Communication

3.4.1 Systems

Several communications systems may be used, which may vary in terms of their quality of service, and may or may not include the ability to detect and repair data file transmission errors automatically. Procedures used to determine which communications system to use for each communication document 'type' should be documented.

eg

Example

An example of differing service quality (but not accuracy, or potential data loss) is where the immediacy of data file delivery is essential and a direct transmission will give this, but an indirect system (such as Internet use) may not. The user will need to choose between what may be differentially charged alternatives.

As an example of differing quality services, a packetized approach such as X25 or TCP/IP may detect lost parts of an electronic communication and ensure retransmission. It will also re-sequence if a packet arrives out of the required order. This type of communications system is in itself lossless.

Many voice and video protocols do not implement these processes. It may be more appropriate to lose a sub-second of a phone call than insert it later in the audio stream out of sequence (the human ear is very good at accommodating lost data, within limits). This type of communication is thus lossy.

Comment – compression algorithms

As discussed previously, some compression algorithms are inherently lossy (e.g. JPEG, MPEG, MP3, etc.); it is also common for communications themselves to be lossy.

VoIP, webcasts, video phones, video surveillance, telemedicine, etc., are all examples that involve communications that have to cope with data loss. Typically, such data loss is caused by network congestion, unplanned or unexpected bandwidth constraints and transmission packets arriving with the recipient out of sequence.

In all these cases the received transaction will differ from that as sent.

Lossy methods should be utilized only if documented quality targets can be demonstrated to be met under anticipated and actual operational conditions. Prior to the use of lossy communications methods, a review and sampling of any impact should be conducted.

The amount of 'loss' can be very significantly affected by loading factors that may be uncontrollable by the parties at either end of the communications link.

Where electronic communications systems require manual intervention to initiate a communication, procedures used should be documented.

> ***Key issue***
>
> **Communications systems should be appropriate to the information transfer requirements.**
>
> **Lossy compression should only be used where it is appropriate to do so.**

3.5 Receipt of communication

3.5.1 General

Where electronic communications systems require procedures to be carried out on receipt of a communication, these procedures should be documented.

Where multiple techniques are employed, particular attention should be paid to ensure that the appropriate technique is used.

3.5.2 Malicious software

To protect from receipt of malicious software (e.g. viruses, macro viruses, worms, Trojan horses, etc.) or unsolicited messages (e.g. spam), appropriate protection software should be installed and kept up to date.

> ***Comment – malware***
>
> **The 2004 DTI Information Security Breaches Survey indicated that 83 per cent of UK large businesses reported receiving emails containing viruses and 67 per cent were infected by at least one virus.**
>
> **Prevention is always better than cure. The cost of recovering from malware is frequently measured in £,000s, not surprising when so many PCs in an organization get infected.**
>
> **'Malware' is short for 'malicious software' and is typically used as a catch-all term to refer to any software designed to cause damage to a single computer, server, or computer network, whether it is a virus, spyware, etc.**
>
> **In addition to malware there is spam (unsolicited commercial messages sent via email) and spim (unsolicited commercial messages sent via an instant messaging system) to worry about. Volumes are massive and continue to grow in spite of the introduction of legislation in various parts of the world.**

Procedures which reduce the possibility of computer viruses and other malicious software being included within information received by electronic communication should be documented. Actions to be taken in the event of an electronic communication being demonstrated (or suspected) of including such malicious software should be documented. This action may include notification back to the sender or receiver, refusal to accept or send the electronic communication, quarantining, disinfecting the electronic communication prior to opening or forwarding.

> ***Key issue***
>
> **Procedures for the protection from malicious software should be implemented.**

3.5.3 Decompression

If data files are received in a compressed format, they will need to be decompressed prior to the presentation to the recipient.

If data files are communicated or stored in a compressed format, decompression processes should be such that the integrity confirmation of received information is not compromised.

> ***Key issue***
>
> **Where compressed files are received, an appropriate decompression procedure should be documented.**

3.5.4 Decryption

Where data files are received in an encrypted form, they may need to be decrypted prior to the presentation to the recipient and/or storage.

Decryption processes should be such that the integrity confirmation of the communicated information is not compromised. The process should only be by/for the individuals or responsible role holders authorized.

> ***Comment – encryption***
>
> **Encryption of communication messages may be to preserve confidentiality whilst in transit over the internet and/or within the sending (or receiving) organization.**
>
> **If the Internet is the concern, then encryption of email is an option worth considering.**
>
> **Messages can be encrypted at an organizational level (e.g. mail server or mail relay) rather than at the level of the individual end user. This will generally mean that there are fewer encryption keys to manage but the message may be in an intelligible form within the organization.**

> *Key issue*
>
> **Where encrypted files are received, an appropriate decryption procedure should be documented.**

3.5.5 Sender identity

Where information has been added to an electronic document prior to communication, which enables the recipient to identify and verify who (individual and/or organization) is the sender of the data file, procedures for the handling of this information should be documented and in accordance with Part 3 of BIP 0008.

> *Key issue*
>
> **A procedure for adding sender identity information where appropriate should be documented.**

3.5.6 Integrity verification

Some systems require that the integrity of a received file is checked before its information content is reviewed, forwarded or stored. Where this is the case, appropriate procedures should be documented.

Where the integrity cannot be checked by the receiving system, consideration should be given to re-communication of the file back to the sender, for integrity verification.

In some applications, electronic files may need to be forwarded to the intended recipient and in some the recipient will collect or fetch a message from an intermediary. Forwarding systems should be such that the integrity of the communicated information is not compromised.

> *Example*
>
> **With IM (instant messaging) and other SIP P2P (peer-to-peer) based systems, when completing a web form or when sending an SMS or a fax, the sender and recipient are in direct contact. There is an end-to-end connection from sender to recipient (often passing through one or more intermediary systems). This differs from internet email, media downloads, file downloads, etc., where the recipient collects the message.**
>
> **With internet email, SMTP (Simple Mail Transfer Protocol) enables the message to be forwarded across the Internet in a number of asynchronous hops to reach, eventually, the recipient's post office. The recipient collects it from the post office using a standard, browser-based interface or with a mail client (such as Outlook,**

Eudora, Thunderbird, etc.) which is an application using a defined interface to the post office; either proprietary or an open standard such as POP3 (Post Office Protocol) or IMAP[5] (Internet Message Access Protocol).

In some systems, file names, digital signatures and MAC codes are used to confirm the integrity of a received communication. Where these systems are used, procedures for dealing with reported errors should be documented.

Comment – message authentication codes (MACs)

Sometimes also called 'keyed hashes', MACs use cryptographic checksums and are an alternative to digital signatures. They can be used to verify the integrity and authenticity of an electronic communication.

MACs are frequently used for file transfers where the communication is between systems inside an organization and is frequently an automated process.

In this case, the sender of a communication and the intended recipient share a secret key (unlike digital signatures where an asymmetric public/private key pair is used). The sender uses the communication and the key to compute the MAC, and sends the MAC along with the communication. When the communication is received, the recipient computes the MAC, and then checks to see if his MAC matches that sent with the message.

If it does, then the recipient knows that the communication is from the other party that knows the secret key and that the communication has not been changed since it was sent.

If a third party does not have the secret key, then even though they may be able to modify the communication, they cannot produce the matching MAC. Therefore any alteration will be detectable.

MACs do not provide any secrecy; if confidentiality is required, the communication should also be encrypted.

A useful source of information relating to MAC codes is the US Federal Information Processing Standards Publication FIPS PUB 198, *The Keyed-Hash Message Authentication Code (HMAC)* published by the National Institute of Standards and Technology (NIST) on 6 March 2002.

The specification in this standard is a generalization of IETF RFC 2104, *HMAC: Keyed-Hashing for Message Authentication*, and the US Standard ANSI X9.71, *Keyed Hash Message Authentication Code* (now withdrawn).

[5] www.xml.org

> ***Key issue***
>
> **Procedures for the verification of the integrity of the received communication should be documented.**

3.5.7 Confirmation of receipt

An electronic communication confirming receipt of an electronic file (including the recipient identity) should be sent to the sender, or to a third party, as proof of delivery if required. The format of confirmation of receipt should be agreed prior to their implementation.

> ***Comment – Simple Object Access Protocol***
>
> **SOAP (Simple Object Access Protocol) is W3C (World Wide Web Consortium) standard protocol for web services. Fundamentally it provides a message exchange envelope for web service payloads. These payloads are frequently in the form of XML documents (which may themselves contain applications data files like Word, Excel, PowerPoint, PDF).**
>
> **SOAP provides the means by which the web service application-specific information may be conveyed in an extensible manner and supports the switching of SOAP messages by providing a full description of the required actions taken by a SOAP node on receiving a SOAP message. Most deployments of web services will require a SOAP envelope to transport the web service payload; they may or may not require the switching features of SOAP.**
>
> **With a SOAP message it is possible to request a delivery receipt and the receiving system is obliged to honour the request. Therefore the sending system can be assured of delivery (or will re-submit the message). In addition, the receiving system can detect duplicate messages and will discard the duplicates.**
>
> **This capability is in direct contrast to SMTP email, where confirmed delivery is not supported.**

> ***Key issue***
>
> **There should be procedures for any manual or automatic process that should be followed in order to verify the receipt of electronic communications.**

3.5.8 Data file format exchange

The recipient should ensure that an electronic file that has been received by communication can be viewed or otherwise accessed, in a form which retains the information content of the electronic document.

eg

Example

Whilst from an evidential perspective it would be nice for the sender and recipient of a particular electronic message to be able to retain identical versions of the messages, this is not always practical.

For example, an email collects metadata during its journey across the Internet (although this may not be seen by the recipient); the email content may also have changed with the addition of a confirmation that it has been scanned for the absence of viruses by a third party service provider contracted to the sender and/or the recipient. Care should also be taken because an email can look very different when viewed with different email clients.

Where a communication cannot be rendered, consideration needs to be given to its acceptability. It may be necessary for an electronic communication to be returned to the sender, with a request for rendering information.

eg

Example

There are three different ways in which communicating counterparties can establish their common capabilities to be able to transfer a message to ensure that it can be successfully interpreted:

1. **prior, out of band, agreement;**
2. **capability negotiation as part of the communication;**
3. **reference to a directory.**

The first method is very simple, it could be as simple as the two parties to the communication agreeing to a separate telephone call to confirm that the message has been received and is accepted.

Typical of the second category is the fax negotiation phase. In the first part of the fax communications connection, before the fax image is transferred, the sending and receiving faxes mutually agree the speed of transfer, the resolution of the scanned or otherwise rasterized image, and the compression mechanism for that image that are supported by both sending and receiving fax systems. IETF RFC 3297 takes this type of approach for content negotiation and capability discovery for Internet messages.

Of the third type, an analogy is the use of Yellow Pages. Web services that are available can be 'discovered', information about the available web service can be obtained from a 'registry', the standard for the web service registry function is UDDI (Universal Description, Discovery and Integration), and the standard for describing web services within the registry is WSDL (Web Service Description Language). WSDL and UDDI provide the equivalent of a 'tailor-made' directory service for the dynamic discovery of web services, such dynamic discovery may be required to provide particular services to end users.

Only after acceptance by the recipient should a confirmation of receipt be sent. Acceptance covers the ability by the named recipient to view the information content of the data file. Care may need to be taken where intermediaries are involved, such as where someone views a data file on behalf of the intended recipient (see below).

eg

Example

The UK e-Government Interoperability Framework (e-GIF) defines the technical policies and specifications governing information flows across government and the public sector. It covers interconnectivity, data integration, e-services access and content management. Many government processes involve interchange of data, underpinning these transactions are common data definitions within the e-GIF, which are defined as XML schemas for use throughout the public sector.

Use of e-GIF ensures that sender and recipient have a common understanding of the contents of an electronically communicated transaction. Whilst applicable to the UK public sector, the principles can be applied to any inter- or intra-organizational transaction.

Where the recipient of a communication is not the intended final recipient, procedures should be implemented which ensure that the final recipient can render the electronic document.

Key issue

Procedures which ensure that the received electronic files can be successfully rendered should be agreed prior to transmission.

3.5.9 Storage

The electronic document that has been received by communication should be stored in accordance with Part 1 of BIP 0008, along with the associated metadata (e.g. data file type, index, sender and recipient identity and address, digital signatures, certificates, receipt confirmation information).

> ***Key issue***
>
> **Store received information in accordance with BIP 0008-1:2004.**

3.6 System maintenance

The electronic communications system should be maintained by qualified and trained personnel to ensure that its performance does not deteriorate.

A maintenance log should be kept, detailing all preventative and corrective maintenance procedures completed.

Procedures for preventative maintenance should be documented. These procedures may be performed by system operators, or by specialized service personnel.

> ***Key issue***
>
> **Where maintenance (corrective or preventative) is required, it should be carried out by trained personnel.**

3.7 Security and protection

The communications systems should operate within the guidelines established in the Duty of care chapter of the Code. This requires the use of security controls appropriate to operational requirements. These controls and associated procedures should be documented.

The physical and operating environments for electronic communications systems should be in accordance with the supplier's recommendations.

Encryption or signature techniques may be used to improve the security and integrity of electronic documents during communications. Where such techniques are used, they should be in accordance with the requirements of Part 3 of BIP 0008.

> ***Key issue***
>
> **Security controls appropriate to the requirements of the information security policy should be implemented.**

3.8 Contracts

Where the exchange of electronic documents is included in an agreement between two parties, any contract document should include clauses relevant to such exchange.

Where both parties agree to comply with the Code, the contract should include (or reference) all relevant documentation required. This should make the contract easier to apply in normal use, and in the event of a dispute. The key requirements identified in 1.2 should be included (or referenced) in the contract, which should be securely stored by the organization in compliance with Part 1 of BIP 0008.

Key issue

Contracts with trading partners should include appropriate clauses to protect the organization during the electronic exchange of information.

3.9 Third parties

Where a third party service provider is used (for example facilities management providers), there should be an appropriate contract in place. The contract should detail the services that are to be used. Such services should comply with the Code.

Example

Contracts should include details on each of the following situations:

- **information security measures;**
- **segregation from other clients' information;**
- **confidentiality measures;**
- **backup and recovery facilities;**
- **identity and authority checking procedures;**
- **service level agreements;**
- **availability of information, processes and procedures, audit trail and expert witness in the event of dispute;**
- **liability;**
- **confirmation of compliance to appropriate Codes of Practice and Standards;**
- **procedures for checking compliance.**

Further details of requirements for contract terms can be found in Part 1 of BIP 0008.

This contract should include agreements which demonstrate that the organization can demonstrate compliance, many years after the event, even if the third party service provider has ceased to trade.

Where third parties provide communications infrastructures (e.g. communications circuits without added value facilities), confirmation and underwriting of service levels concerning network availability and commitments to deliver data unaltered and unobserved needs to be sought.

Where the third party service provider sub-contracts some or all of the provision, details of the procedures used by the sub-contractor should be documented and responsibility for service provision clearly understood by all parties.

The organization should include in their agreement with the third party service provider the rights to all relevant information held and procedures used in the event of:

- the third party service provider ceasing to trade;
- the organization, at the end of the agreement, deciding to use an alternative third party service provider.

The controls over the exercise of these rights should be defined in the agreement with the third party service provider.

Wherever service level agreements are part of the contractual provision of the communications system service, reporting against these levels should be provided. This may need to be on an immediate basis rather than after the event.

Further details of the use and management of trusted third parties can be found in BS ISO/IEC TR 14516:2002.

Key issue

When using third parties to provide electronic communications systems or services, appropriate contracts should be in place to manage the facilities used.

3.10 Standardized documents

Organizations may use 'skeleton' documents or 'templates' for the creation of personalized documents for communication purposes. Where it is likely that there may be a challenge to the authenticity of such a document, the sender should be able to reconstruct the communicated document. This requires that the original skeleton or template is stored, together with information regarding the version used for any particular created document.

Where standardized documents are modified and communicated, the original documents should be held in compliance with Part 1 of BIP 0008. The content of these documents should be managed using a version control system, to enable appropriate records to be kept of changes made to these documents.

All versions of such documents should be stored in accordance with the organization's retention policy.

Comment – XML schemas

XML schemas express shared vocabularies and allow machines to carry out rules made by people. They provide a means for defining the structure, content and semantics of XML documents.

In addition to e-GIF, there are many XML schema definitions publicly available such as ebXML (Electronic Business using eXtensible Markup Language). It is a modular suite of specifications designed to enable enterprises of any size and in any geographical location to conduct business over the Internet. Using ebXML, companies have a standardized method to exchange business messages, conduct trading relationships, communicate data in common terms and to define and register business processes.

These XML schemas effectively address the same inter-organizational interoperability requirements as the standards used in EDI, such as Tradacom or Edifact.

It is quite acceptable for trading partners to mutually agree to a private EDI format or XML schema, however, if they chose to do so there is an ongoing documentation and maintenance task that is likely to be an unproductive use of resources.

Key issue

Where templates/skeleton documents are used, they should be managed and stored using the same procedures as the documents that used them during their creation.

3.11 Version control

All hardware, software and procedural documentation used in conjunction with the Code should be maintained under a version control system.

Such systems should include the keeping of appropriate records of changes made and should enable relevant information about the configuration of the electronic communications system at any time in the past to be reviewed.

Key issue

Keep records of all procedural and process documentation in accordance with a retention policy. This is to enable the configuration and use of the system at any point in the past to be demonstrated.

3.12 Change control

Where changes to automated processes occur, an appropriate change control procedure should be followed. Such processes should be tested prior to live implementation and audited. Records should be retained which demonstrate the proper implementation of change control procedures.

eg

Example

Where script changes for automated file transfers are implemented, the new scripts should be fully tested prior to their implementation.

Key issue

Keep records of all procedure and process changes, including an audit trail of testing and implementation.

Chapter 4 Enabling technologies

4.1 Management overview

It is important to utilize reliable and trustworthy technology to facilitate electronic communications. Each part of the system needs to be chosen with care, taking into account the possible need to demonstrate 'proper' and 'appropriate' working of the system some time in the future. This demonstration may need to encompass both the technology itself and the methods by which it was configured and used. The 'enabling technologies' chapter covers particular aspects of technology (for example, the communications hardware used) as well as critical aspects of configuration (for example, how access to the system is managed).

Thus, implementers of electronic communications systems need to ensure that they have been designed in accordance with the requirements of the Code. This chapter contains details of processes that need to be implemented, enabling the procedures defined in Chapter 3 to be applied.

4.2 System description manual

4.2.1 Documentation

A description of hardware, software and network elements that comprise the electronic communications system is required. This should include details of system configuration. The documentation should be structured so that details of the system at any time during the period of its use may be readily accessed. This may be achieved by creating a new version of the manual every time there is a change, or by including a 'change control' section in the manual. What is important is that there is a clear description of the system as it was at a particular time in the past.

For systems already in operation, information communicated by the system prior to the introduction of the Code cannot be considered as meeting its provisions unless the controls and procedures described in the Code have been in place from the time of communicating that information.

Where the information communications policy requires conformance to particular national and/or international standards, the system description manual should include a section demonstrating compliance with those standards. This enables system auditors to check the performance and reliability of the system against these standards.

> **Key issue**
>
> **A system description manual should be made available, containing details of (or reference to other relevant documentation) all technology related issues relevant to the information management system at any point in time.**
>
> **Document any compliance to standards methodology implemented.**

4.2.2 Content

The system description manual should include the topics listed below:

Subject	*Technology*	*Section*
General issues	Details of the issues related to compliant communications systems	4.3
Communications systems	Details of the systems in use	4.4
Access levels	Configuration of user access management tools	4.5
Identity	Processes for confirming the identity of sender and recipient	4.6
Identification of documents	Ensuring that communicated documents are correctly identified	4.7
Communication initiation	Processes for initiating communications	4.8
Integrity checking Processes which	ensure the integrity of communicated information	4.9
Authentication	Authenticating the sender and recipient	4.10
Receipt confirmation	Dealing with the confirmation of receipt	4.11
Temporary storage Storing information	prior to write to final storage	4.12
Time considerations	Dealing with time issues	4.13
Error handling	Dealing with errors in communications systems	4.14

4.3 General issues

There are many types of electronic communications systems, for example:

- email systems;
- instant messaging (IM) and other P2P (peer-to-peer) 'presence' based systems;
- fax systems;
- point-to-point corporate systems;
- internal network systems.

Each of these has its own facilities and functionality. Relevant information is needed regarding the operation of all systems used for electronic communications.

For each system, the following issues need to be addressed:

- delivery and/or receipt may be at the organization, at specific premises or locations, within the system, or direct to and/or from the users, or any combination;
- internal corporate networks, either as a means of delivery to users connected to it or as a means of breakout to lessen carrier call charges, should be included in the communications system;
- the use of public message switching services should be included. The significance of any potential time delay in a document reaching the intended recipient should be documented. Such delays can be caused by:
  - message switching and prioritization;
  - network congestion;
  - message collection.
- similar delays can be caused where Internet browser, internal email or other similar delivery systems are used;
- the use of integrity control, confirmation of delivery and/or receipt systems.

eg

Example

For example, although a fax-to-fax machine communication may appear to be immediate there may be considerable delay before it is received by the intended party, due to memory caching and/or paper handling procedures.

Comment – P2P file sharing

Instant messaging and many peer-to-peer file sharing systems raise significant security issues because of the way they use HTTP-S to create encrypted channels that pass potentially unseen content through firewalls and other security defence components.

It was reported in early 2005 that the first malware exploiting this vulnerability had been detected. Using P2P networks like Kazaa and eMule the malware uses features of Microsoft Digital Rights Management (and included in a wide range of their standard software) to create a secure channel whereby inappropriate or damaging software can be loaded, unnoticed by perimeter defences. These 'stealth mode' malware Trojan horses leverage the feature in the DRM software whereby if a copyright licence is not available on the user's system, a secure link is created to download a licence; in this case the download was not a licence but a damaging Trojan horse payload.

Even if not compromising security, organizations should be careful about allowing users to make use of public IM or P2P file downloading systems. A survey in late 2004 indicated that of the Gnutella P2P traffic on the internet, 47 per cent related to pornography and 97 per cent infringed copyright. If this is through the organization's system, the organization may have unwittingly become responsible under the terms of vicarious liability.

4.4 Communications systems

Documentation should include all types of electronic communications systems available for use. It should identify (by reference or by documentation) attributes at any relevant historical time as associated with a particular electronic communication.

Where a service provider (or facilities management provider) is used, details of (or references to) their relevant systems should be documented. In this case, much of the required documentation will be able to be sourced from the service provider. Note though that the service provider may change the details of the service and commitments to quality from time to time, without required notification.

It may be necessary to store copies of any service provider documentation rather than just referring to it.

Key issue

All communications systems in use or used in the past, together with communicated information still stored, need to be fully documented.

4.5 Access levels

4.5.1 General

There should be documentation available which details all levels of access available to the electronic communications systems. These levels are typically as follows:

- system manager/administrator;
- user;
- system engineer.

The documentation should include access methods whereby only authorized staff can use or administer the system.

Where the communications system utilizes encryption techniques to ensure that access to confidential data is restricted, access to keys should be controlled appropriately and documented.

Key issue

Access levels to communications systems should be documented.

4.5.2 Access levels and third parties

Where third parties are given access to communications systems, details of their access levels should be documented. These access levels may include:

- authorized client staff;
- authorized third party service provider staff;
- system manager;
- system engineer.

Where service provider staff have access to communications systems, terms of the controls/checks applied to such staff should be agreed and documented. Controls/checks applied to such staff should be such as to ensure that they do not misrepresent or otherwise misuse the systems.

Where service provider staff have access to communications systems, the service provider should verify that all such staff have entered into suitable non-disclosure and other confidentiality agreements.

Where communications are with a third party archiving organization, details of processes which ensure that access is allowed only to their own authorized information should be documented. This requires that there should be appropriate processes for the secure identification of individuals requiring access, and the management of authority levels for new/changed/deleted users.

Key issue

Where third parties are involved, access levels allocated to third party staff should be controlled.

4.6 Identity authentication

There should be documented processes which identify the senders and recipients of communicated documents. More details of these processes can be found in Part 3 of BIP 0008.

Where electronic communication headers and/or confirmation of receipt fields are used, they should contain details of the person/application and/or the organization who sent the document.

Where an organization is involved in the sending and/or receiving of an electronic communication, the identity of the organization[6] should be included.

NOTE: This in itself does not prove the source of the document.

If passwords, PINs, biometrics and/or certified digital signatures are used, singularly or in combination, this will generally enhance the certainty that the sender/recipient are who they purport to be (see Part 3 of BIP 0008).

[6] Where appropriate, BS ISO 6523-1:1998, should be used for such identifications.

The issuance of keys and certificates will also provide supporting evidence of sender/recipient identity (see Part 3 of BIP 0008).

Where network information is provided by the electronic communications system, this should be retained [e.g. calling line identifier (CLI), universal resource indicator (URL)]. Care should be taken as to the value of this information, as it may be limited where such information has not been disclosed or when forwarding and relaying is involved.

Key issue

See Part 3 of BIP 0008 for details of identity authentication.

4.7 Identification of documents

For subsequent distinguishing recognition purposes, each communicated document should be allocated an unambiguous identifier by the sending system. This identifier should be communicated with the document.

Identifiers should be specific to the sending organization and consideration should be given to the risks inherent in an identifier not being unique.

Identifiers should be allocated such that, should a dispute arise concerning communication timing, prior and subsequent electronic communication timings can be used in support as necessary.

The sender, recipient and subject of the document should be clearly identified and communicated with the document.

The processes whereby additional metadata is added automatically and/or manually to an electronic communication should be documented. This additional metadata may (for example) be additional indexing information or version numbering, which will aid subsequent storage and retrieval of the electronic communication.

Definition

Metadata is data about data or, more fully, a description of the content and form of any resource. Examples include a shopping catalogue, describing the price, size, colour, brand and features of the items for sale, or the 'properties' section of an electronic file, giving the size, format, date created, creator and title of the file. Metadata can be added to, or attached to, a web page, file or database, or any other information resource. Metadata can be machine-readable, giving software applications the data they need to interpret the information held on a file, or it can be designed more for human interaction, listing the creator, title, subject and other data needed to find or manage the resource.

The e-Government Metadata Standard (e-GMS) lays down the elements, refinements and encoding schemes to be used by government officers when creating metadata for their information resources or when designing search systems for information systems. The e-GMS forms part of the e-GIF. The e-GMS is required to ensure maximum consistency of metadata across public sector organizations.

Key issue

Methods for the unique identification of communicated documents should be implemented.

4.8 Communication initiation

The effective communication initiation time for an electronic document is when it leaves the sender in an electronic form. The sender may be an individual, a business unit or the application that originated the electronic document. Where communication is between organizations, then the sender should be unambiguously linked to the originating organization, and the initiation time is when the document is communicated by the organization.

The processes used to record when electronic communication is initiated should be documented. A time and date stamp should be added to the document at the time of communication and communicated with the document.

NOTE: A date and time stamp from a PC on a network is unlikely to be the actual communicated time unless it is connected to the carrier directly.

Where the 'actual' time of a communication event is important, the use of 'trusted time' should be considered (see box).

Definition

'Trusted time' is time that is certified to be traceable to the legal time source for the application in which it is being used and is not forgeable either at the time of initial use or at any time in the future.

To help in this area, the IETF have published a document entitled *Internet X.509 Public Key Infrastructure Time-Stamp Protocol (TSP)* (RFC 3161) which describes the format of a request sent to a time-stamping authority (TSA) and of the response that is returned. It also establishes several security-relevant requirements for TSA operation, with regards to processing requests to generate responses.

A time-stamping service supports assertions of proof that a datum existed before a particular time. A TSA may be operated as a trusted third party service, though other operational models may be appropriate, e.g. an organization might require a TSA for internal time-stamping purposes.

Another useful source is the Technical Specification published by the European Telecommunications Standards Institute entitled *Electronic Signatures and Infrastructures (ESI); Policy requirements for time-stamping authorities* (ETSI TS 102 023).

Where a break in communication occurs, the reconnected time and date may also need to be recorded and communicated.

Key issue

Processes used in the initiation of communication should be documented. The process for the addition of time of initiation should be included.

4.9 Integrity checks

4.9.1 Sending

The processes used for ensuring the integrity of the communicated information during the 'send' operation should be documented.

Where the communications system is inherently lossless, checksums may be employed. They should be applied to the electronic document as part of the communications system.

A checksum may be computed to include the date/time sent, such that if the document date is changed, then the checksum would change. If, on receipt, the checksum does not match the document, then document integrity has been compromised. This fact should be highlighted and re-transmission processes should be invoked.

Example

Whilst from an evidential perspective it would be nice for both the sender and the recipient to be able to present an identical electronic message, this is not always possible.

For example, an email collects metadata during its journey across the Internet (although this may not be seen by the recipient); the email content may also have changed with the addition of a confirmation that it has been scanned for the absence of viruses by a third party service provider contracted to the sender and/or the recipient. Care should also be taken because an email can look very different when viewed with different email clients.

Cryptographic checksums (MAC) or digital signatures can provide additional strength for this control.

Comment – cryptography

The cryptographic hash and signature algorithms are used in combination with cryptographic keys (and padding algorithms) to produce digital signatures.

Signature algorithms include:

- DSA (digital signature algorithm);
- RSA (Rivest, Shamir and Adleman algorithm) as specified in the US Standard ANSI X9.31-1998;
- ECDSA (elliptic curve DSA) as specified in the US Standard ANSI X9.62-1998.

Cryptographic hash functions are detailed in BS ISO/IEC 10118-3:2003, *Information technology — Security techniques — Hash-functions — Part 3: Dedicated hash-functions.* Typical of such hash functions are:

- MD5;
- RipeMD16;

Secure hash algorithm (SHA); which has a number of variants:

- SHA-1;
- SHA-256;
- SHA-384;
- SHA-512

[as defined in the Federal Information Processing Standards Publication (FIPS PUB) 180-2].

The European Telecommunications Standards Institute has published a Special Report entitled *Electronic Signatures and Infrastructures (ESI); Algorithms and Parameters for Secure Electronic Signatures* (ETSI SR 002 176).

In addition, the World Wide Web Consortium (W3C) and the Internet Engineering Task Force (IETF) have jointly created a standard that describes processing rules and syntax for the use of digital signatures in XML documents.

A fundamental feature of XML signature is the ability to sign only specific portions of the XML tree rather than the complete document. This flexibility will be critical in situations where it is important to ensure the integrity of certain portions of an XML document, while leaving open the possibility for other portions of the document to change. Consider, for example, a signed XML form received by a user for completion. If the signature were over the full XML form, any change by the user to the default form values would invalidate the original signature.

Where cryptographic techniques are employed for confirmation of integrity or identity, it is important that cryptographic keys are managed appropriately and not compromised. The actions to be taken and reporting to be followed in the event of actual or suspected compromise must be documented.

This process is frequently referred to as key management. As the entire digital signature and encryption operations are dependent upon the security of the keys, there should be rigorous processes in place to manage them.

Clearly, in the area of managing keys, roles and responsibilities should be defined. Typically there should be segregation of roles. The staff involved in any aspect of key management should not be those who run the business from day to day, or have access to development systems or production systems. In many organizations, all staff apart from those involved are obliged to leave the room where keys are being changed.

Sometimes, as in message authentication codes, there is a requirement for secret keys to be sent to each participant for authentication of transmitted data. In this case, the keys themselves should be encrypted or transferred outside the normal communications system.

Example

If a secret key used for a MAC is compromised and known to a third party, then that third party could modify the message and the recipient would be unaware of the changes. The recipient would also be unaware that the datafile did not actually come from the expected sender because the MAC itself is genuine.

Key issue

Methods of managing cryptographic keys used for checking the integrity of electronic communications should be documented. This should include actions to be taken in the event of compromise.

Comment – cryptographic keys

The two components required to encrypt data are an algorithm and a key. The algorithm is widely known but the key is kept secret.

In a symmetric cryptosystem, the same key is used for encryption and decryption. In an asymmetric cryptosystem, however, the key used for decryption is different from the key used for encryption; these are known as key pairs. Encryption is performed with the public key of the recipient and decryption with the recipient's private key.

NOTE: For digital signature purposes the signing process uses the signer's private key, the signature is checked with the corresponding public key.

Where a certification authority is used, it is the public key that is certified, not the private key.

Keys should, whenever possible, be distributed by electronic means, enciphered under previously established higher-level keys. There comes a point, of course, when no higher-level key exists and it is then necessary to establish the key manually.

A common way of doing this is to split the key into several parts (components) and entrust the parts to two people to reduce risks of compromise. The two people put in half a key each, each going in a secure room alone to enter their part. That ensures no single person can ever normally know the key (other than where collusion is occurring). It is important that none of the key parts should contain enough information to reveal anything about the key itself.

A problem frequently occurs when it is necessary to re-enter a key from its components in this way. This is always an emergency situation and it is often found that one of the key component holders cannot be found. For this reason sometimes the key components are distributed among three key holders in such a way that only two of them need to be present.

For example, if there are three key parts (P1, P2, P3) and three key holders on the staff (S1, S2, S3) then S1 could have (P1, P2), S2 could have (P2, P3) and S3 could have (P3, P1).

In this arrangement, any two of the three key holders would be sufficient.

In many systems, the components are held on smart cards.

Where the communications system is inherently prone to data loss (lossy), such as many real time voice systems (where the human ear is better able to cope with slight gaps than data delivered fully, but out of natural sequence), alternative approaches to integrity are likely to be adopted. Whilst it might be possible to apply a checksum to the electronic communication prior to archiving, it cannot be applied 'on the wire' as what was sent and what was received may be different bit-streams.

In these cases, it is important that the communication document is recorded accurately and retained and that the amount of 'data loss' can be shown to be within demonstrable and previously sampled limits that meet the defined acceptance criteria.

Communications systems should report if 'data loss' exceeds pre-defined thresholds and appropriate pre-defined processes should be invoked.

> **Key issue**
>
> **Methods of checking the integrity of sent electronic communications should be documented. This should include both lossless and lossy communications systems.**

4.9.2 Receiving

The processes used for ensuring the integrity of the communicated information during the 'receive' operation should be documented.

Where an integrity-checking system was used during the send operation (for example, the addition of a checksum), then the receiving system should confirm the integrity using appropriate technology.

> **Key issue**
>
> **Where integrity checking systems were added to electronic communications when they were sent, appropriate technologies should be used when they are received, to confirm integrity.**

4.9.3 Sending data to archives

Technologies used for the initiation and control of transfer of information between the organization and an archive, whether the archive is operated in-house or by a third party service provider, should be documented.

There are two main approaches to data archiving:

- send every data file to the archive at the same time as it is sent to the recipient, or when a confirmation of receipt is received;
- send the data file to the archive, for them to forward it to the ultimate recipient (this is sometimes called an 'in-line notary').

> **Comment**
>
> **Where a notary service provider is used, it should be in compliance with the Code for each of the separate communications (the first between sender and notary, the second between notary and recipient).**

Such capabilities as provided by these approaches may be used selectively. Where proof of authenticity of identity of sender and/or recipient is required, cryptographic controls (e.g. digital signatures) will frequently be used.

The method of ensuring that received and subsequently stored electronic information is identical to that originally sent should be documented. Such integrity checks should include situations where the data files have been moved from one storage device to another, and where recovery from system failure has occurred.

Key issue

Technologies used for managing the transfer of information to electronic archives should be documented.

4.10 Sender and recipient authentication

Sender and recipient authentication can be achieved in a number of ways, each of which may be of value to both parties. Techniques used may vary depending upon the document type being communicated. This is covered in more detail in Part 3 of BIP 0008.

Typical techniques include:

- sender or recipient identification trusted;
- sender or recipient identification guaranteed;
- sender or recipient identification verified by third party;
- electronic document re-communication to sender and confirmation received (possibly using alternate communications methods);
- electronic document stored or notarized via or by a trusted third party.

Techniques used for sender and recipient authentication should be documented.

Proving the recipient identity may in certain circumstances be unimportant. Frequently, electronic communication confirmation of identity of an organization rather than an individual will suffice to meet user requirements.

Key issue

See Part 3 for more details of sender/recipient authentication methodology.

4.11 Receipt confirmation

4.11.1 General

Upon receipt of an electronic document, a confirmation of receipt should normally be sent to the sender. Receipt confirmation should be at least at the organizational level. Where appropriate, a personal receipt from the intended recipient should be sent. A time received identifier should be used, with the ability to distinguish between organization receipt and personal receipt, where appropriate.

This confirmation should include both details of the communication document sent and an unambiguous confirmation of receipt, i.e. it should contain document details and recipient details.

> *Example*
>
> **The way in which a receipt is communicated from recipient to sender depends on the communication methods used.**
>
> **For example, this may be as an integral part of the communication transaction itself as in the case of IM or fax, where it is the final part of the transmission between the two systems.**
>
> **In other examples, such as SMTP email or SOAP, the receipt is a separate, asynchronous, message that has sufficient metadata to allow the sending system to associate it with the original message.**

The receipt confirmation may be an electronically-communicated document in its own right and, as such, it should be handled in accordance with the Code.

> *Key issue*
>
> **The processes used for receipt confirmation should be documented.**

4.11.2 Document details

The following information should be included with a communicated document, to enable a confirmation of receipt to be communicated to the sender:

1. sender and recipient identity;
2. subject (and/or other information) of electronic communication;
3. unambiguous electronic communication identification;
4. sender time and date stamp;
5. sender's checksum on the file and associated metadata (may be a digital signature).

> *Key issue*
>
> **Listed above is the information to be sent with an electronic communication (or included within it), such that a receipt confirmation message can be generated.**

4.11.3 Receipt details

The following additional information should be returned to the sender and stored, both by the sender and the recipient, in such a way that it is linked with the communicated document:

1. sender and recipient identity;
2. unambiguous electronic communication identification (to enable the sender to match the receipt to the appropriate electronic communication);

3. sender's checksum on the file and associated metadata;
4. received time and date stamp;
5. checksum for the specific receipt covering the above data, including the checksum on the received electronic communication (may be a digital signature).

> ***Key issue***
>
> **Listed above is the information to be used to generate a receipt confirmation message.**

4.12 Interim or temporary document storage

The processes whereby a sent or received data file, and confirmation of sending and receipt are written to storage should be documented.

The controls described in Part 1 of BIP 0008 should be implemented to facilitate legally admissible storage.

Where indexing processes are automated, processes used on receipt of such an electronic file should be documented. Such processes should ensure that documents include and/or have sufficient indexing information to enable effective subsequent retrieval.

> ***Key issue***
>
> **Details of any temporary storage processes should be documented.**

4.13 Time considerations

The processes implemented for the recording of electronic communication date and time details should be documented. Consideration should be given to the format of this especially when information is communicated across time zone boundaries.

Timings can be as follows:

- where documents are communicated in real time;
- where documents are stored and then communicated at a later time;
- where there is a difference between document receipt by an organization and by the person.

For 'store and forward' systems, or where receipt by a person is later than that by the organization, controls implemented to ensure that the document is not amended during its storage should be referenced.

Where the actual time that an event occurred is important, the use of trusted time from a third party service provider should be considered.

Where available, and where time is important, processes for the recording of confirmed, trusted timestamps should be documented.

> ***Key issue***
>
> **Where time is important, accurate time stamps are necessary.**

4.14 Error handling processes

The processes used in error handling systems should be documented. They should be implemented to identify and correct received data errors.

Should an interruption occur during an electronic communication, either the communication should be cancelled and re-initiated, or a process should be implemented to provide continuation communication with clear referencing to the first electronic communication where the service break occurred.

> ***Key issue***
>
> **The handling of transmission errors should be documented.**

Chapter 5 Audit trails

5.1 Management overview

When preparing information for use as evidence, it is often necessary to provide further supporting information. This information may include details such as date of communication of the information, details of movement of the information from medium to medium, and evidence of the controlled operation of the system. These details are known as 'audit trail' information.

This audit trail information is needed to enable the working of the system to be demonstrated, as well as the progress of information through the system. Audit trails need to be comprehensive and properly looked after, as without it the integrity and authenticity, and thus the evidential weight of the communicated information, could be called into question.

5.2 Audit trails

5.2.1 Historical records

The audit trail as defined for the Code consists of the aggregate of the information necessary to provide a historical record of all significant events associated with communicated information. As such it covers the answers to all the classic questions concerning the provenance of any electronic information that has been subject to electronic communications:

- Who?
- What?
- Where?
- When?
- Why?
- How?

These audit trail details can be split into two categories:

- system (including the hardware platform(s), applications and operating software, configuration, processes and procedures);
- communicated information.

In most organizations, the audit trail will consist of a collection of system- and operator-generated logs.

It is essential that system clocks be synchronized with an accurate time source to ensure that times recorded in audit trails are consistent and reliable.

5.2.2 Audit trail data

Audit trails should be:

- managed;
- inclusive;
- secure.

5.2.3 Content

Records should be kept of historical activities or events that may need to be reconstructed in the future, as additional evidence to support communicated electronic documents.

Audit trails should contain the sufficient and necessary information to provide evidence of the authenticity of communicated electronic documents.

> *Key issue*
>
> **Audit trails should contain sufficient information to be able to demonstrate all necessary historical activities relating to the system and to the data communicated.**

5.2.4 Access

There are frequently a number of departments (or individuals) within an organization (or external to the organization) including those representing user, audit and legal functions, which may need access to specific parts of audit trail information. This access should be controlled, to reduce the possibility of compromise.

Users of third party archives need to ensure that audit trail information as described in this section is being created by the third party, and is available to them in a timely and controlled manner.

> *Key issue*
>
> **Relevant personnel should have access to audit trail data commensurate with their role.**

5.3 Managing audit trails

5.3.1 General

The audit trail needs to be properly managed, as it may be of critical importance to the organization. All claims of compliance to organizational policies may be discredited if the audit trail is not treated correctly and cannot be interpreted unambiguously.

> ***Key issue***
>
> **Ensure that the audit trail data is authentic, accessible, sufficiently comprehensive and understandable.**

5.3.2 Storage and retention

The storage of audit trail data is a topic often not included in an organization's electronic communications policies. As they are frequently created automatically, and infrequently accessed, they are forgotten and thus not subject to adequate control.

To ensure that all relevant audit trail data is stored, 'audit trail data' should be included as a specific document 'type' in the policy document. It should be stored for at least as long as the information to which it refers is stored.

Some systems control the size of audit trail data files by the use of 'looping', which sets the maximum size for the data file, and when this size is reached, new data overwrites the oldest data in the file. Thus, old audit trail data is lost. This process may not be in compliance with required retention periods.

There should be procedures which identify circumstances when an audit trail data file becomes full, and take action to retain data as required by the retention policy.

Where an organization is working within an ISO 9000 environment, audit trail data relating to compliance with the quality management system are typically destroyed after a short period of time. This is not the case with audit trail data from electronic communications systems, which should be stored for the same period as that of the data to which it relates.

> ***Key issue***
>
> **Ensure that audit trail data is retained for at least the same period as that of the data to which it relates.**

5.3.3 Format

Frequently, when an organization wants to automate its computer operations environment, it makes use of operating system logs to monitor the system for specific events or error conditions.

At an application level, ensuring that the application provider uses standard error messages, typically agreed with the organization during the design stage, enables application status conditions to be monitored also.

For example, if an application reads invalid data from a file, rather than just aborting the program with nobody aware of what happened (until the users raise a support call), if the program writes a status message to an error/system log, in an agreed format, the monitoring software will detect this and notify the appropriate area.

These notifications are an important trigger to investigate the continued, proper operation of the system. The entries into the error system log that caused the monitoring software to raise the alert should be part of the audit trail and should be controlled in accordance with this Code.

> ***Key issue***
>
> **Use audit trail formats which enable easy interpretation, both by system users and by automated monitoring tools.**

5.3.4 Access and interpretation

Access to audit trail information needs to be controlled. In some applications, access may only be needed infrequently, and thus it is important that the interpretation procedures are documented. As audit trail data may be inspected by authorized external personnel (such as auditors) who have little or no familiarity with the system, interpretation procedures should be understandable by non-technical users.

Access to the audit trail should itself be recorded in the audit trail.

> ***Key issue***
>
> **There should be documented procedures which are followed when audit trail data needs to be accessed and interpreted.**

5.3.5 Audit trail information

For all audit trail data, it should be possible to identify the process involved and the date and time of the event.

Depending on its importance, date and time information may be stored on a batch or individual event basis. Where audit trail data is stored manually by an operator, it may be impractical and unnecessary to create audit trail data on a per communication basis. For example, when undertaking the communication of a number of electronic files, it may be sufficient to document the time at which the communication of a batch of documents started and ended. It may suffice to document simply when the operator started and ended work, provided it is possible to identify subsequently which operator prepared which electronic files.

> ***Key issue***
>
> **Audit trail data should include a date and time stamp.**
>
> **It may be appropriate to audit at the batch level rather than the individual document level, in some parts of the capture and storage processes.**

5.3.6 Compliance

The Compliance Workbook, BIP 0009-2[7], may be used to enable a comprehensive assessment to be made of the user's system for conformity with the Code, and to help identify which parts of the Code are relevant.

Compliance with the Code should be claimed only if all recommendations, as stated in the Workbook, have been met, or justifications for any non-applicable recommendations documented. Compliance with the Code should be claimed via an authorized statement, examples of which are shown in 5.3.7.

Electronic communications systems should be audited on a regular basis to ensure that the provisions of the Code are met and that the approved procedures are being adhered to. This audit should review audit trail data that is produced on a regular basis for evidence of ongoing, continuous compliance.

The person identified in 1.2.7 as being responsible for maintaining compliance with the Code should review the results of each audit and document/implement a plan to address any non-compliances which should be re-audited.

A record of compliance with the Code should be maintained, as part of the audit trail. This record should include details of which recommendations are not considered relevant, and justifications for these decisions.

Where compliance with previous editions of the Code has been claimed, copies of those editions should be retained as part of the compliance audit trail.

Where any change is made to the electronic communications system, or to relevant procedures, which affects compliance with the Code, a new audit of compliance should be undertaken.

Auditing may be carried out by authorized and trained in-house staff or by suitable third parties.

> ***Key issue***
>
> **Use the Compliance Workbook (BIP 0009-2) to audit and document compliance with the Code.**
>
> **Re-audit on a regular basis, and during major system change.**

[7] In preparation.

5.3.7 Statement of compliance

5.3.7.1 General

Compliance with the Code should be claimed using statements which differ depending upon whether:

- the end user organization is claiming compliance;
- the system supplier is claiming that a system can be used in a compliant manner;
- the third party, acting as auditor, is confirming a compliance status.

Recommended text is given below, for use in compliance statements. Alternative text may be used but legal advice should be sought to ensure its suitability.

5.3.7.2 End user organizations

Individuals who or organizations that conduct audits of their own electronic communications systems may certify compliance via the following statement:

'[insert name of organization] confirms that the [insert name or other identification for the system] electronic communications system is operated in compliance with BSI BIP 0008-2:2005.'

The statement should be signed by an officer of the organization, stating their position.

NOTE: the policy document should identify the individual or position within the organization authorized to sign statements of compliance with the Code (see 1.2.7).

5.3.7.3 System integrators and developers

Individuals who or organizations that integrate/develop/supply electronic communications systems may certify that their systems may be used in a compliant manner via the following statement:

'The [insert name or other identification for the system] electronic communications system supplied by [insert name of integrator/developer/supplier] provides all facilities necessary for a user of this system for implementation in compliance with BSI BIP 0008-2:2005.'

The statement should be signed by an officer of the supplier organization, stating their position.

5.3.7.4 System auditors

Individuals or organizations that conduct audits of electronic communications systems may certify compliance via the following statement:

'[insert name or auditing organization or individual] has assessed the [insert name or other identification for the system] electronic communications system operated by [insert name of organization] for compliance with BSI BIP 0008-2:2005 and hereby certifies its compliance.'

The statement should be signed by an officer of the auditing organization, stating their position.

> ***Key issue***
>
> **Claim compliance using an authorized statement.**

5.4 Audit trail content

5.4.1 General

The audit trail content is critical, as it can be used to audit such activities as preparation and sending and receiving of electronic communications. Thus, the audit trail needs to include a record of all relevant activities related to the systems. If any significant activity is not audited, then the whole audit trail can be discredited and, as a direct result, all or any electronic communications will also be able to be discredited.

Thus, technologies for providing electronic communications systems should be chosen with audit trail requirements in mind. This may result in technologies being rejected that may otherwise have appeared suitable for a particular application.

> ***Key issue***
>
> **When choosing electronic communications systems, consider suitable audit trail functionality as a basic system requirement.**

5.4.2 Generation

Audit trail data should, as far as practicable, be generated automatically by the system, and the system description manual (see 4.2) should describe the processes. In this case, the data should be created and stored immediately following the event that is being audited.

Where audit trail data is not generated automatically by the system, procedures for its manual (or other) generation should be implemented. In this case, the data should be created as soon as possible after the event that is being audited. For example, if the record is of when an operator of an electronic communications system started work, the time should be recorded before work actually starts. If the record is of when preparation of a particular batch of electronic documents was started, the time should be recorded just before the preparation of that batch commences.

It should not be possible to amend any audit trail data. Deletion should only be possible in accordance with the organization's retention policy.

> ***Key issue***
>
> **Audit trail data should be generated automatically wherever possible.**
>
> **It should not be possible to alter audit trails.**

5.4.3 System audit trail

The system audit trail should store details of significant events, primarily to enable users to determine the status of the system at a relevant time in the past. There should be sufficient information to enable the user to determine whether the system was 'working normally' when a particular event occurred.

Where information has been converted from one format to another, as part of the electronic communications system, details of the conversion processes should be stored in the audit trail.

> ***Key issue***
>
> **System audit trails should be able to demonstrate 'proper working' of the systems.**
>
> **They should also be able to demonstrate the successful completion of format conversion processes.**

5.5 Communicated information

5.5.1 General

The audit trail should contain the following information where relevant:

1. time when electronic communication was initiated;
2. time when the inbound receipt was effected;
3. time when personal receipt was effected.

In some applications, a requirement for confirmed, trusted timestamps is key. Such information should be recorded in the audit trail.

5.5.2 Route details

The audit trail should contain the following information where relevant:

1. communication initiator (person or application);
2. initiation hardware;
3. communication server;
4. protocols used;
5. carrier(s) used;
6. receiving server;
7. communication receiver (person or application).

5.5.3 Storage requirements

Where there is a requirement for intermediate storage, sufficient audit information should be stored to enable such time and route details as are required to be made available.

> ***Key issue***
>
> **Store audit trail information related to ensure that time and route details can be determined.**

5.5.4 Date and time

Each audit trail data record should have an associated date and time which relates to the date and time of the electronic communications event. This information should be sufficiently accurate that a subsequent investigation can determine the train of events.

The date and time will normally be that of the creation of the audit trail data, but if this creation is made essentially contemporaneously with the event which is being audited, the time will be, to all intents and purposes, that of the event itself.

Where a date and time stamp is applied automatically by the system, all changes to the system clock should be recorded in the audit trail. Such changes need to be suitably authorized and may be necessary to adjust for daylight saving time or inaccuracy of the clocks.

Where the actual time that an event occurred is important, the use of trusted time should be considered (see 4.13).

It may be appropriate to link audit information to the information to which it refers, by the use of digital signatures, MACs or other forms of cryptographic checksums.

> ***Key issue***
>
> **Ensure sufficient accuracy of date and time for the application in question.**

5.6 Security

5.6.1 General

The audit trail needs to be secure. If an audit record can be maliciously or inadvertently altered or counterfeited, then the whole audit trail may be discredited and as a direct result, all or any communicated information held within the system may also be able to be discredited.

5.6.2 Access

Audit trail information needs to be accessed by authorized operators at relevant times. In some applications, access may only be needed on an ad hoc basis, and thus it is important that the access and interpretation procedures are documented.

There should be procedures for the secure management of audit trail access and interpretation.

Audit trail data should be available for inspection by authorized external personnel (such as auditors) who have little or no familiarity with the system.

Access to the audit trail should, itself, be audited.

> ***Key issue***
>
> **Keep audit trails secure, with audited access only.**

5.6.3 Integrity and protection

If the authenticity of communicated electronic documents is questioned, the integrity of the audit trail may be fundamental in establishing the authenticity, and thus the evidential weight of this information. If the possibility exists that the audit trail data could be modified, this will reduce the evidential weight of any information to which these records apply.

The audit trail should be kept at the level of security appropriate to preventing any change to any data within it, and in accordance with the organization's information security policy (as well as the retention policy).

The audit trail should be subject to equivalent internal records management policies and procedures as other 'vital records' of the organization.

Secure backup copies of the audit trail should be kept, including automated and manual audit trail data.

Where file recovery procedures have been implemented as part of the communications systems, sufficient audit trail data should be stored to demonstrate that the recovery did not affect information authenticity.

For least risk, store audit trail data on 'write once read many' WORM media. If a rewritable medium is used, then additional procedures need to be implemented to prevent changes being made. The use of magnetic tape will make it relatively difficult to modify data, as magnetic tape is normally a serially written medium.

If audit trail data has been modified, then any such modification should be audited.

Paper documents used for audit trail data should be removed frequently from the place of use and stored securely. The longer a document used for audit trail data (e.g. operator logs) is left in a relatively insecure place, for example at a workstation, the higher the risk of tampering. Users need to assess such risk when using paper for audit trail records. Where paper documents are used, electronic copies of them should be stored on an information management system (in accordance with Part 1 of BIP 0008).

> ***Key issue***
>
> **Wherever possible, store audit trail data in an un-modifiable form.**
>
> **Where this is not possible, use security measures to ensure that it is not modified.**

Chapter 6 Unstructured message considerations

6.1 General

Where organizations seek to maintain systems for the electronic communication of unstructured messages in compliance with the Code, additional details should be included within the policy document (see 1.2). Such systems are a significant form of inter-company messaging and include email, fax, short message service (SMS) and instant messaging (IM) systems.

The guidelines in this chapter set out procedures which may be reviewed and, where appropriate, incorporated into the policy document.

6.2 Policy objectives

The policy document should cover the following key objectives:

1. creation of electronic message text;
2. policy regarding unsolicited messages (e.g. spam, spim, etc.);
3. copyright and ownership;
4. storage and archiving of electronic messages;
5. receipt of electronic messages.

Typical contents of these sections are detailed below.

The organization should develop a policy appropriate to its own circumstances and should ensure that it is properly authorized, under appropriate change and version control, and demonstrably understood by and accepted by users as appropriate.

Comment

Some confusion could occur here over the term 'policy'. There may be multiple policies that may appear to overlap or conflict.

The organization should have a policy that is readily available to all staff that makes their individual roles and responsibilities clear. This is critically important for unstructured communications such as email,

fax, SMS and IM. This may typically be part of the staff handbook or Internet acceptable use policy.

The organization should have a policy for managing electronic communications and this may, or may not, be readily available to all staff. This policy may refer to the staff handbook or Internet acceptable use policy to avoid duplication.

Key issue

The policy document should be extended to cover unstructured message communications, such as email, fax, SMS and IM.

6.3 Creation

Email, fax, SMS and IM are particularly informal forms of electronic communications, and are classified as 'unstructured'. Typically, individual members of staff are able to include content and decide layout without corporate guidance. As such and without special attention, these unstructured messages can result in communications standards below those normally expected by the organization. In order to manage these issues, guidance is needed in how to create unstructured messages.

Thus, the policy document should include the following:

1. how to address messages, especially to individuals/organizations outside the organization;
2. importance of clear, single subject identification, as electronic messages are often dealt with based on this;
3. writing standards (short, precise, to the point);
4. spelling (often overlooked, spellcheckers should be used);
5. circulation (often overdone, should be only on need-to-know basis);
6. open/closed copying (large lists of those copied may be unnecessary);
7. illegal or potentially damaging electronic message content (e.g. libel, defamation, obscene, copyright breach);
8. attachments (ensuring they can be read by recipients);
9. contracts (if contracts are concluded by electronic communication, take care – some contracts need to be in paper form to be enforceable in certain jurisdictions. Take legal advice. If in doubt, send a paper copy for each party to sign);
10. electronic business. Arrangements for electronic business need to be carefully considered. As a baseline, the following need to be taken into account:
    - information retention requirements;
    - communications requirements;
    - proof of identity;
    - payment, or commitment to pay, for a specific product or service.

Comment

It is important to make people who have access to electronic message systems aware of the (lack of) confidentiality of messages sent in an unencrypted form.

It may be illegal to send some types of electronic message (e.g. those containing pornography). Other contents may have potentially damaging effects if disclosed to/intercepted by a third party (e.g. those containing defamatory statements).

As a general rule, users and organizations should understand that unencrypted electronic messages are just as easy for anyone to read as an open 'postcard' through the conventional postal systems; with unencrypted messages there is no equivalent of the physical envelope that protects the content from inappropriate disclosure or from tampering. If an electronic message needs to be communicated in a confidential manner, then encryption is one technique that could be used.

In addition, the following issues should be included in the policy document where relevant:

1. personal passwords, or alternate identity authentication (e.g. biometrics, identity tokens etc.);
2. encryption policy – define when encryption should be used and ensure the intended recipient can decrypt;
3. lodging encryption keys or transactions with third parties (see Part 3 of BIP 0008);
4. international considerations – respect date, time of day, unit of measurement of the recipient and be aware of legal protection issues (e.g. trademarks);
5. jargon – email, SMS and IM use their own jargon. Assess when and where it is acceptable;
6. staff training policy – detail training provisions;
7. what procedures should be followed if an illegal or improper electronic communication is found.

Key issue

Rules regarding the creation of unstructured messages should be devised and implemented.

6.4 Spamming, filtering and viruses

The sending of unsolicited bulk messages by emails (so called 'spam'), SMS or IM ('spim') is illegal in certain jurisdictions. To guard against unlawful activities in this arena, appropriate policies should be devised and implemented.

Policies should include:

1. adequate safeguards to ensure that unwanted, unsolicited messages do not reach employees;
2. awareness and agreement by employees of actions to be taken on receipt of unsolicited messages;
3. requirement for procedures which ensure that illegal unsolicited messages are not generated;
4. requirement for procedures to be actioned if unsolicited messages have been sent or may be received.

Filtering techniques are designed to stop unwanted incoming and/or outgoing messages by filtering on their content. These techniques will, for example, identify foul or pornographic language and delete or quarantine such messages. These techniques can also, however, if too vigorously applied, filter out genuine electronic content.

The organization's employees and contractors should be aware of the use of these technologies and work within the rules applied.

Viruses are computer software which may cause major damage to any computing system that they come into contact with. They are often received through incoming messages (email is currently a major source of such malicious software but it is spreading to other messaging forms like IM, and to mobile phones, PDAs and other connected devices).

The organization's employees and contractors should be made aware of the danger from viruses and other malware received through electronic messages. They should be required to comply with the organization's policy for the detection and defence against message borne viruses and other malware.

Virus and other malware control software will not automatically identify all viruses, as new ones are continually being created. It is thus important to ensure that such systems are regularly updated.

The organization's employees and contractors should:

1. be aware of the risks with the various forms of spam and malware;
2. take appropriate preventative action where necessary;
3. immediately report any suspected spam, virus or other malware.

Key issue

Protection against the various forms of unsolicited messages and malware should be implemented and kept up to date.

6.5 Copyright and personal use

6.5.1 Policy

Employees have rights and responsibilities concerning electronic messaging and so does the organization. A policy should be developed in relation to these rights, to meet organizational needs. This policy should clearly define the rights of the organization and of the individual, especially in the area of the use of the organization's messaging resources for personal matters.

This policy should be carefully drafted and in accordance with general organizational policies with regards to their employees, as too rigorous a policy may be unenforceable and may lead to employee unrest, whereas too lenient a policy may encourage abuse. The policy should be written in such a way that it is understood by all employees.

It may be appropriate to take legal advice when drawing up this policy.

In order to ensure implementation of the policy, compliance should be a part of the employee's contract of employment. When sub-contractors and other third parties use the organization's messaging facilities, an agreement relating to their use should be part of the related contract.

6.5.2 Copyright

Copyright of electronic messages typically resides with the sender of the message unless agreed otherwise. Most organizations may wish to place ownership under their own control. Thus, appropriate agreements on this issue need to be included in the employee's contract of employment, or other equivalent document.

6.5.3 Privacy

Privacy rights of the individual sender and recipient will vary from country to country. Within the UK, these are typically found in the Data Protection Act 1998 and the Regulation of Investigatory Powers Act 2000. Electronic messaging systems operating across national borders may give rise to additional privacy issues relating to the different countries involved.

In the absence of an explicitly accepted policy, users may have a legal right to assume that their communications will remain private.

To meet corporate requirements, organizations will typically need to have rights of access to electronic communications handled by their employees. To ensure that this is within their legal rights, they may need to gain explicit prior agreement to this from their employees and sub-contractors.

6.5.4 Personal use

It may be appropriate to allow limited personal use of electronic messaging systems. Such rights and responsibilities should be defined by the inclusion of appropriate words in the employee's contract of employment.

Organizations should be aware that, if an employee with personal use of their electronic messaging system becomes the subject of an investigation (e.g. criminal or civil), the organization may be required to provide evidence of the employee's use of the system and may be responsible for the effects of its employee's actions.

6.5.5 Monitoring

With the ownership of copyright come related responsibilities. The organization should assess its risks in this area and formulate an appropriate message monitoring control policy.

At one extreme, companies may be legally required to monitor electronic messages, for example to ensure that illegal messages are not created and sent. At the other extreme, regulations may preclude monitoring, for example in the personal correspondence with the employee's trades union representative. For international messaging, the legal situation in each country may need to be reviewed. Finally, the type of businesses involved and risks being taken needs to be put in the balance.

To manage these issues, organizations should have a clear, implemented policy for the monitoring of electronic messages.

To ensure that employees are able to understand the policy in detail, it should be drafted in simple terms, and training and/or other awareness methods should be available as and when required. To avoid friction with employees in the development of such a policy, it may be appropriate to include them in development of the policy and encourage their contribution to creative ideas in the use of company messaging technology.

6.5.6 Breaches, procedures and penalties

The policy should set out the employee position should a breach occur, the procedures to be followed and penalties which may ensue. Typical penalties range from a simple 'ticking off' to dismissal. Such penalties should be included in the policy document, and should be applied irrespective of the employee's position within the organization.

Key issue

Policies for the use of electronic messaging for personal use, including copyright and monitoring issues, should be included in the policy document.

6.6 Retention and destruction

Much electronic messaging activity is informal, and will not be required for long term retention/record keeping/archiving purposes. Some messages, however, may by law be required to be kept for a minimum period.

To ensure availability and integrity of retained messages, the retention should be under the terms of Part 1 of BIP 0008.

Where an organization has a corporate retention policy, electronic messages should be included within that policy. They should not be included as a specific single 'document type'. A method of classifying individual messages and then allocating them an appropriate retention period should be the normal process.

Example

Electronic message categorization may best be managed by enabling the employee to identify messages that need to be kept beyond a short retention period. Those for longer storage should then be copied to an electronic storage system outside the messaging system.

This process should be a 'mirror' of the related paper-based system. When a message on paper is received, it is either dealt with and stored 'on the file', or it is dealt with and discarded immediately. An example of the first action is where an application form for a service is received. The second action could be appropriate for a notice of a meeting.

The following issues should be considered and, if necessary, risk assessments should be made before policies are implemented:

1. normal retention periods for electronic messages may be relatively short (30/90 days);
2. longer retention periods could possibly create higher risks for the organization;
3. conversely, longer retention periods could lower risks by protecting the organization against claims that the content was inappropriate or defamatory – remember that the sender or recipient who was once trusted may have a copy of the message and may now be an adversary;
4. some electronic messages will need long term retention/archive for legal or regulatory purposes – these types of documents/electronic mail need to be clearly identified and staff need to be made aware of this. This applies to both sent and received electronic messages, which should be retained according to the policy;
5. disclosure orders – be aware that authenticated copies of appropriate electronic messages may need to be disclosed in court (see Part 1 of BIP 0008 for details of authentication methods);
6. deletion processes need to ensure that the original, together with all copies, backups and external copies (e.g. laptops, mobile phones and PDAs) are deleted.

Key issue

Corporate retention policies should be applied to electronic messaging systems. A policy of short retention periods for all messages may not meet legal requirements.

6.7 Receipt

Electronic messages in the form of email, fax, SMS and/or IM lend themselves to rapid communications. Senders typically expect an immediate reply. They assume that delivery has been achieved and that the message has been read, within a short time interval from their send time. This may not be the case, due to delays in transmission or the unavailability of the recipient to deal with the message. Messages may not be delivered, due to addressing errors, system failure or filtering mechanisms.

Some messaging systems include a 'proof of delivery' option, whereby the recipient is asked to confirm receipt. Whilst the receipt of such a confirmation message may be trustworthy, the absence of such a receipt may not be reliable evidence as to either delivery or non-delivery.

Policies for use in relation to received electronic messages should consider receipt from a customer service viewpoint, with typical issues to be covered, including:

- use of filtering systems to exclude unsolicited messages and malware from electronic communications – over-filtering may, however, result in lost orders!;
- verification of identity of sender;
- verification of receipt and/or reading;
- prompt and courteous replies (where needed);
- refer to the sender's subject or reference – develop policy on sending incoming electronic messages with replies as appropriate;
- if necessary, forward to appropriate parties – if necessary seek permission to forward. Note that copyright resides with the sender (author);
- productivity policy – electronic messaging can be very time consuming;
- assess value of subject previewing and/or set times for handling to improve productivity;
- consider the role of a gatekeeper to monitor/direct incoming electronic messages.

Key issue

Policies on the handling of received messages should bear in mind the expectations of the sender.

Annex A Example electronic communications policy

This annex contains an example 'electronic communications policy document'. It can be used as a draft upon which an organization's policy can be based.

XYZABC Limited

ABC project

Policy document for compliance with *Code of practice for legal admissibility and evidential weight of information communicated electronically* (Reference BSI document: BIP 0008-2:2005)

Approved by:	
Name:	
Position:	
Date:	

1. Scope

This document covers the information management policies implemented within the XYZABC Limited electronic information communications systems. This policy conforms to the recommendations of the Code of practice for legal admissibility and evidential weight of information communicated electronically (BSI BIP 0008-2:2005).

- HIJ electronic information communications system;
- KLM Internet web service;
- PQR automated reporting system;
- XYZABC Limited email system;
- XYZABC Limited facsimile server system and stand-alone facsimile machines.

These electronic information communications systems are described in a system description manual (Ref: SD02). Procedures for the use of the systems are described in a procedures manual (Ref: PM02).

2. Information covered

Communicated information covered by this policy document relates to those messages used in relation to all aspects of electronic communications for XYZABC Limited. Documents included within the scope of this policy are detailed in the communication schedule, Annex A.

XYZABC Limited does not operate an information classification system, as all information is regarded as having the same security level.

3. File formats

All communicated information (messages, message metadata and message attachments) are communicated in formats as described in the communications schedule, Annex A.

4. Standards

All electronic information communication within XYZABC Limited is communicated in compliance with BSI BIP 0008-2:2005, together with any referenced national and/or international standards.

All electronic information communication within XYZABC Limited is stored in compliance with BSI BIP 0008-2:2005.

5. Data file and document communication

5.1 General

The communications schedule, given in Annex A, has been agreed within XYZABC Limited to cover legal and operational requirements consistent with the status of being a public limited company.

All communications systems used within XYZABC Limited are the property of XYZABC Limited and are provided to help meet the business aims and responsibilities of XYZABC Limited; staff, employees, contractors and others utilizing these systems have no expectation of privacy relating to their use of these communications systems.

All document and message types communicated, structured and unstructured, are detailed in the communication schedule as defined in Annex A of this policy document.

5.2 Structured

This section deals with electronic documents communicated with:

- HIJ electronic information communications system;
- KLM Internet web service;
- PQR automated reporting system.

The structured documents communicated are detailed in the communication schedule as defined in Annex A of this policy document. For each document type the following will be considered:

- data file formats;
- compression and encryption;
- pre-transmission processes;
- communications channel used;
- post-transmission processes;
- integrity confirmation;
- confirmation of identity of sender/recipient;
- conformation of delivery/receipt;
- responsibility for message.

In all cases where a document has been sent or received, it will be retained and, at the appropriate time, destroyed in compliance with BSI BIP 0008-1:2004.

5.3 Unstructured

This section deals with communications messages which are sent or received on an ad hoc basis. This includes person-to-person email and fax communications as detailed in Annex A.

NOTE: email and fax generated automatically from PQR system is included under the terms of the previous section.

The unstructured documents communicated are detailed in the communication schedule as defined in Annex A of this policy document.

Email and fax systems are provided to facilitate effective business communication and may be used for limited personal use as defined in the staff handbook.

Unstructured messages by email and fax can be highly effective, if properly used, or highly damaging, if improperly used. Guidelines for proper use and sanctions that will be imposed for improper use are detailed in the Internet acceptable use policy.

These guidelines include, but are not restricted to:

- creation of messages;
- virus and other malware protection;

- unsolicited bulk messages;
- copyright, ownership and monitoring;
- receipt of and reply to messages;
- storage and retention of messages (in compliance with BSI BIP 0008-1:2004);
- personal use.

In addition, other criteria to be applied to specific message types is as detailed in the communications schedule, Annex A. This includes but is not restricted to when and how encryption is to be used, when and how message integrity is confirmed, when and how identity of sender and recipient are checked, whether proof of delivery is required, what pre- and post-transmission checks should be performed.

Use of email systems, other than those provided by XYZABC Limited, is not allowed and any use of other email systems on XYZABC systems or premises is in breach of the terms detailed in the staff handbook that form part of the contract of employment.

Instant messaging, other than that of the restricted users of the MNO system, is not allowed and any use on XYZABC systems or premises is in breach of the terms detailed in the staff handbook that form part of the contract of employment.

6. Responsibilities

This policy document should be reviewed annually under the control of the Company Secretary. Where changes are agreed, they are implemented using the change control procedures (Ref: CC01).

This policy and any revisions to it, should be approved by the Board of Directors of XYZABC Limited prior to its implementation.

The maintenance of compliance with BSI BIP 0008-2:2005 is the responsibility of the Head of Internal Audit.

7. Legal advice sought

XYZABC Limited have sought and obtained agreement for this communication policy and the communication schedule detailed in Annex A of this document.

8. Duty of care

XYZ Limited has a duty to keep secure and accurate original documentation, or authentic copies of them. This is achieved by:

- implementing this policy document;
- implementing an information security policy;
- ensuring that only trained staff have access to the system;
- ensuring that acceptable quality control procedures are implemented;
- ensuring that XYZABC Limited legal advisors are consulted, and appropriate actions taken.

Annex B References

BSI standards publications

BRITISH STANDARDS INSTITUTION, London

BSI Publications are available from Customer Services, Sales Department, 389 Chiswick High Road, London W4 4AL.

Tel: 020-8996-9001; Fax: 020-8996-7001

PD 0006:1995, *Technical guide to JPEG — Digital compression of photographic images.*

BIP 0008-1:2004, *Code of practice for legal admissibility and evidential weight of information stored electronically.*

BIP 0008-3:2005, *Code of practice for legal admissibility and evidential weight for linking electronic identity to documents.*

BIP 0009-2, *Code of practice for legal admissibility and evidential weight of information communicated electronically — Compliance workbook.*[8]

PD 0010:1997, *Principles of Good Practice for Information Management.*

BIP 0071[9], *Information Security Management Systems (ISMS) certification — Guidelines on requirements and preparation for certification based on ISO/IEC 27001:2005 (BS 7799-2:2002 revised).*

BIP 0072, *Are you ready for ISO/IEC 27001:2005 Information Security Management Systems (ISMS) Audits?*

BIP 0073, *Guide to the implementation and auditing of Information Security Management Systems (ISMS) controls.*

BS ISO 6523-1:1998, *Information technology — Structure for the identification of organizations and organization parts — Part 1: Identification of organization identification schemes.*

ISO 8879:1986, *Information Processing — Text and Office Systems — Standard*

---

[8] In preparation.

[9] PD 3001, PD 3003 and PD 3004 are to be revised in 2005 to create BIP 0071, BIP 0072 and BIP 0073 respectively. PD 3002 and PD 3005 are to be withdrawn on publication of BS 7799-3.

Generalized Markup Language (SGML).

BS EN ISO 9001:2000, *Quality management systems — Requirements.*

BS ISO/IEC 10118-3:2003, *Information technology — Security techniques — Hash-functions — Part 3: Dedicated hash-functions.*

BS EN ISO 14001:2004, *Environmental management systems — Requirements with guidance for use.*

BS ISO/IEC TR 14516:2002, *Information technology — Security techniques — Guidelines for the use and management of trusted third party services.*

BS ISO/IEC 17799 (BS 7799-1), *Information technology — Security techniques — Code of practice for information security management.*

BS ISO/IEC 27001 (BS 7799-2), *Information technology — Security techniques — Information security management systems — Requirements.*[10]

Other publications

GREAT BRITAIN. Anti-terrorism, Crime and Security Act 2001. London: The Stationery Office.

GREAT BRITAIN. Regulation of Investigatory Powers Act 2000. London: The Stationery Office.

GREAT BRITAIN. Data Protection Act 1998. London: The Stationery Office.

RFC 2104 - *HMAC: Keyed-Hashing for Message Authentication.* IETF, 1997.

RFC 3161 - *Internet X.509 Public Key Infrastructure Time-Stamp Protocol (TSP).* IETF, 2001.

RFC 3297 - *Content Negotiation for Messaging Services based on Email.* IETF, 2002.

RFC 3851 - *Secure/Multipurpose Internet Mail Extensions (S/MIME) Version 3.1 Message Specification.* IETF, 2004.

IETF/W3C, *XML-Signature Syntax and Processing.* World Wide Web Consortium (W3C) and the Internet Engineering Task Force (IETF), 2002. Available at: http://www.w3.org/TR/xmldsig-core/

Federal Information Processing Standards Publication (FIPS PUB) 180-2, *Secure Hash Signature Standard (SHS).* Gaithersburg: National Institute of Standards and Technology (NIST), 2002. Available at: http://csrc.nist.gov/publications/fips/fips180-2/fips180-2.pdf

Federal Information Processing Standards Publication (FIPS PUB) 198, *The Keyed-Hash Message Authentication Code (HMAC).* Gaithersburg: National Institute of Standards and Technology (NIST), 2002. Available at: http://csrc.nist.gov/publications/fips/fips198/fips-198a.pdf

Special Report (SR) 002 176, *Electronic Signatures and Infrastructures (ESI); Algorithms and Parameters for Secure Electronic Signatures.* European Telecommunications Standards Institute (ETSI), 2003.

ETSI TS 102 023, *Electronic Signatures and Infrastructures (ESI); Policy requirements for time-stamping authorities.* European Telecommunications Standards Institute (ETSI), 2003.

---

[10] Publication expected in autumn 2005.

ANSI X9.31-1998, *Digital Signatures Using Reversible Public Key Cryptography for the Financial Services Industry (rDSA).* American National Standards Institute (ANSI).

ANSI X9.62-1998. *Public Key Cryptography for the Financial Services Industry: The Elliptic Curve Digital Signature Algorithm (ECDSA).* American National Standards Institute (ANSI).